CHAPTER 1

INTRODUCTION

The Not-Too-Distant Future: The Combined Joint Task Force ABLE Scenario

Combined Joint Task Force ABLE was activated on 18 February 1999 to assist the Government of Indonesia in reducing human suffering following weeks of devastating floods and landslides. Over 1,200 American soldiers, airmen, sailors, marines, government representatives, and civilians joined with over 500 of their counterparts representing 27 nations in this massive humanitarian assistance effort. Most of these personnel were bivouacked at Camp Angel, an impromptu collection of buildings and tents just outside of the capital city of Jakarta.

On the night of the first of March, a large truck bearing the markings of the International Committee of the Red Cross slowly approached the entrance to Camp Angel. This was not unusual; similar trucks had made routine such trips to the compound since the beginning of the crisis. Suddenly the driver gunned the engine and the truck rammed the gate. Unerringly the truck raced into the interior of the camp where it slammed into the Combined Operations Center and exploded. With an explosive force later estimated by the Federal Bureau of Investigation (FBI) at the equivalent of 20,000 pounds of TNT, the center of the compound was obliterated. Instantly, 212 Americans, (including 198 military members) and 37 representatives of other countries died.

Simultaneously an Internet announcement by the Islamic Jihad-General Command claimed responsibility for the bombing. Their communiqué stated this blow was a strike for freedom against the illegitimate and imperialistic domination of the Great Satan, the United States of America, and their stooges. They promised further death and destruction to the infidel as they purified the world for the faithful. They vowed to continue to strike at times and locations of their choosing until all the unbelievers are dead.[1]

More chilling, within a few days survivors and emergency services personnel who had responded to the disaster began to sicken and die. An analysis showed the bomb contained a deadly biological agent that was released by the force of the explosion. By the time authorities contained the plague, over 1,000 more people had died in this attack--the deadliest terrorist attack recorded.

In addition to the death and destruction, the task force commander was relieved of command and court-martialed for dereliction of duty. In his defense, the commander contended he followed the applicable antiterrorism (AT) doctrine "in spirit and in deed" and that any fault should lie in the failure of that doctrine! Was that truly the case, and is the doctrine inherently flawed? Or did the commander simply fail in the judicious application of that doctrine? Does the doctrine lie at the heart of the problem, the collective inability to achieve success with respect to AT activities to protect U.S. troops? Clearly, the U.S. military institution owes commanders the doctrinal tools they need to succeed.

Introduction

Is the scenario presented in the preceding section a bit farfetched? Perhaps, but observe the parallel with the October 1983 terrorist attack that destroyed the U.S. Marine Headquarters at the Beirut International Airport, an event indelibly inscribed on the institutional memory of the U.S. Marine Corps. Apparently, not everyone paid heed to the lessons of that tragedy for the June 1996 bombing of Khobar Towers in Saudi Arabia was like watching the replay of a bad drama on television.

There are many other incidents, too numerous to mention, that share certain common characteristics. First, members of the Armed Forces of the United States of America were killed or wounded in these attacks. Second, in each instance a military commander was responsible for the safety and security of those people. Third, the commanders failed either through acts of

2

omission or commission, to safeguard their troops. And fourth, there was a range of AT doctrine in force at the time of these attacks.

The last point is most significant; the role of AT doctrine must be considered and evaluated to preclude such attacks. In short, doctrine is the institutional body of knowledge that military forces use to accomplish their assigned mission. In that doctrine, commanders search for a method to take a proactive approach to the present-day dangerous environment and anticipated potential problems. In other words, the military must learn from past mistakes and anticipate future requirements, thus preventing another Beirut Airport or Khobar Towers disaster.

The ambient environment surrounding the military members, the varying type and degree of threat, and the commanders' control over the surroundings characterized the attacks mentioned above. In other words, commanders must first understand their environment and the ambient threat. They can then meet that threat with the doctrine, tools, and authority granted to them. Incomplete intelligence or lack of requisite authority can easily lead to a realm of uncertainty that can confront commanders in their decisions on how to apply antiterrorism doctrine. That is not unusual; military commanders have long been accustomed to compensating for varying degrees of uncertainty in their decision making. Even so, something went very wrong in each of these cases, and it resulted in the death of American military personnel. Was the doctrine to blame?

In this post-Cold War world, America has seen a retrenchment of military forces from large numbers stationed abroad to a continental-based force that is deployed in times of crisis or need. Increasingly, due to institutional changes in how the American military operates and budget-driven declining force structure, these deployments take the form of joint (meaning more than one military service) and multinational operations under the command of a joint commander. Often, these commanders are expected to work with functionaries of other governmental agencies, representatives of the host government and other interested nations, nongovernmental organizations, and the media. While synergy is certainly a benefit in this type of arrangement, the

3

www.ingramcontent.com/pod-product-compliance
Lightning Source LLC
Chambersburg PA
CBHW081226280526
45787CB00006B/2537

structure is inherently more complex than ever before in history. Even within the United States, commanders must work within an environment of cooperation with other federal, state, county, and local officials, not to mention the private agencies and organizations that abound. In any environment and regardless of whether there is an ongoing overt war, commanders face a difficult and growing threat of terrorism. Dealing with the threat of terrorism is just one of a commander's burdens, but one that has catastrophic implications if overlooked. AT doctrine must be capable of operating in the most complicated of environments.

In the final analysis, one inescapable conclusion can be reached. Terrorism continues to pose a clear and present danger to the members of the armed forces of the United States, at home and abroad. "U.S. military and DoD [Department of Defense] civilians face a continuous threat from a multitude of terrorists, organizations, and individuals using terrorist tactics for criminal, or political gain."[2] Religious and issue-specific terrorism (e.g., environmental or antiabortion) is on the rise. U.S. troops may be specifically targeted or simply be at the wrong place at the wrong time. As the people in the military are the most valuable resource of all, it is incumbent upon all military commanders to protect their personnel in order to maintain the combat capability of their organizations. Force protection is the encompassing concept and antiterrorism is a large component of that concept. In today's environment, the commander that neglects force protection issues will most likely not remain a commander very long.

This study seeks to discover what is wrong with the doctrinal process from a macroscopic view. Before that can be done, a key assumption must be made. Namely, it is essential to identify the commander as the friendly center of gravity, "the hub of all power and movement upon which everything depends,"[3] in the collective antiterrorism effort. As General Shalikashvili, former Chairman of the Joint Chiefs of Staff (CJCS), said regarding antiterrorism efforts, "the key remains you--the commander."[4]

Commanders are provided doctrine, organization, training, leadership, information, and materiel with which to combat terrorism. If these six elements are considered as decisive points, "the keys to getting at centers of gravity,"[5] it follows that the most significant decisive point leading to the defined center of gravity is the AT doctrine available to the commander. Why? Because doctrine is "the authoritative guide to how Army forces fight wars and conduct operations other than wars."[6] The other services express similar sentiments about the role of doctrine. While some caveats apply to this philosophy (and will be explored in turn), this approach will be used as the foundation for this study.

To summarize, given the changing deployment characteristics of American forces, the change in the international environment of the foreseeable future, and complex domestic considerations, commanders will face a continuing, significant, and credible danger to their forces from terrorist attacks. In this battle to safeguard American soldiers, sailors, airmen, and marines, commanders must be given the best possible doctrine; doctrine that analyzes the lessons of the past, teaches the current generation of leaders and troops, and guides succeeding generations safely through the terrorist minefields. Despite the considerable effort following in the wake of the Khobar Towers attack, guidance to commanders in the form of antiterrorism doctrine is not sufficient to counter the threat. Therefore the hypothetical scenario outlined in the beginning of this paper is quite possible but not acceptable.

The Thesis Statement

To counter the continuing and growing terrorist threat, what doctrinal improvements can be made to better prepare commanders to reduce the vulnerability of their forces to terrorist attacks?

The Research Question

Accordingly, this study is designed to answer the following question: What are the shortfalls and recommended reforms for current antiterrorism doctrine?

5

Subordinate Questions

In order to answer the primary question, the thesis must build on a series of lesser questions. First the doctrine and its prominent characteristics must be defined. This will establish a baseline of common understanding for the rest of the study. Once that is determined, then the question of whether or not the current doctrine can be described in the context of a fundamental, environmental, and organizational model should be asked. Simultaneously using that same hierarchical structure, the study will determine if the content of the doctrine addresses specified strategic, operational, and tactical requirements. This framework will allow concurrent analysis of the structure and the content of the institutional doctrine.

There are two parts of the AT environment that are critical, the threat and the commander's authority to deal with that threat. To set the stage properly, the study must ask what constitutes the anticipated terrorist threat and how intelligence is required to counter the threat. By gaining an appreciation for the evolution of the terrorist threat, an objective judgment can be made as to the validity of the doctrine to allow for that change.

Commanders' authority is a large component of AT doctrine, but it has its limits. To fully appreciate the environment, the doctrinal restrictions, constraints, and limits placed on commanders' authority must be delineated. Analysis will show how those restrictions are overcome or provide recommendations for change.

Traditionally, the concept of security has been a part of military combat operations; today's environment demands security in every facet of life, combat or noncombat. This study must determine if a complete understanding of the concept of security and its relation to AT permeates the doctrine and by extension the commander's mindset.

To add real-world relevance, the study will apply the current doctrine to two selected historical cases. Using the documented findings published in the wake of those cases, the study

6

will ask if the current doctrine would be reasonably capable of preventing the incident. When all these elements are then combined, a coherent picture of AT doctrinal reform emerges.

Context of the Problem and the Research Question

Undeniably, terrorism is a clear and present danger to the national interests of the United States. As President Clinton wrote in *A National Security Strategy for a New Century*, "we must continue to move strongly to counter growing dangers to our security: weapons of mass destruction, *terrorism*, [emphasis mine] international crime."[7]

The study of terrorism is a fascinating journey into human psychology. Terrorism can be the pinnacle of political determinism, religious fealty, or personal self-expression. Depending on one's point of view it can be either vilified or worshipped. Terrorism is nothing new; individuals and groups have used terror, abstract violence, and coercion for ages. In today's military newspeak, it can arguably be considered the original "asymmetric threat." Seemingly, no nation or people are immune from it. Terrorism has ruined lives, destroyed families and lands, and has toppled governments and nations. The inability of the Carter administration to effectively deal with the Iranian hostage crisis helped to ensure their 1980 reelection defeat. Terrorism has elevated the terrorist to political supremacy (e.g., Yassir Arafat) and has been the basis for the founding of new states (the ethnic cleansing in Bosnia-Herzegovina).

In 1996, there were 296 acts of international terrorism documented by the Department of State (DoS) as the agency charged by U.S. law to track terrorist activity. The total number of casualties was one of the highest ever recorded: 311 people were killed and 2,652 were injured. A single event (a bombing in Sri Lanka) killed 90 people and injured more than 1,400 others.[8]

Virtually every authority accepts that terrorism can be combated by offensive means (counterterrorism) or by defensive means (antiterrorism). Coping with after-the-fact terrorism is generally fraught with peril, with the potential cost in lives, resources, and national prestige. Unfortunately, this reactive approach has been the historical method of response during the 1970s and through the early 1980s. In the U.S., elite military units and civilian organizations, such as the FBI Hostage Rescue Team, have been glorified in the media and popular culture. Waiting until an event happens and then responding to the threat means surrendering the initiative to the enemy. It is usually more desirable to prevent the activity (and the crisis that generally accompanies such an act) from occurring in the first place. That is the domain of antiterrorism and is the focus of this study.

Definitions

It is the perverse nature of language that the same word can mean different things to different people. Consequently, it is important to specify clear definitions for the terms that will be used in this presentation. It is important to note that consensus on some terminology is not universal; there is considerable argument in sociological and academic circles on a suitable definition of terrorism itself. This confusion has led to a less-than-total response on the part of the affected governments. Lieutenant Commander Steven Presley, U.S. Navy, has compiled a very insightful listing of diverse definitions of terrorism in his thesis, "Rise of Domestic Terrorism and Its Relation to United States Armed Forces."[9] However, for the purposes of this study, the Department of Defense definition of terrorism is suitable. DoD calls terrorism, "the calculated use of unlawful violence in inculcate fear; intended to coerce or to intimidate governments of societies in the pursuit of goals that are generally political, religious, or ideological."[10]

Finding a suitable definition for doctrine is similarly difficult. It is important to recognize at the outset that this is part of the problem with AT doctrine; the different military services have different views on the roles and functions of doctrine. As this is an integral part of the study, further discussion will remain as part of the analysis of chapter 4.

Fortunately, the other terms used in this study don't elicit as much debate. The Department of Defense uses the umbrella term "force protection" in relation to all the measures designed to prevent nonbattle casualties. This study will use the term force protection in the following context: "Security program designed to protect soldiers, civilian employees, family members, facilities, and equipment, in all locations and situations, accomplished through planned and integrated application of combatting terrorism, physical security, operations security, personal protective services, and supported by intelligence, counterintelligence, and other security programs."[11]

In order to narrow the focus, this study defines combatting terrorism as: "Actions, including antiterrorism (defensive measures taken to reduce vulnerability to terrorist acts) and counterterrorism (offensive measures taken to prevent, deter, and respond to terrorism), taken to oppose terrorism throughout the entire threat spectrum."[12]

An expansion on the discussion of AT indicates it is "Defensive measures used to reduce the vulnerability of individuals and property to terrorist acts, to include limited response and containment by local military forces."[13]

Commanders are those individuals specified under public law as being designated by the Secretary of Defense responsible for the protection or security of military installations and equipment.[14] It is important to note that the DoD interpretation of this definition also includes a provision for installations or activities that are not headed by a military commander, such as leased commercial offices that houses military recruiters. In this case, "the 'designated commander' is the military commander in the chain of command immediately above such installation or activity."[15] This is critical in a situation like the 1995 Murrah Federal Building bombing where military members and DoD civilians were working outside a traditional military installation.

Limitations

Combating terrorism involves certain aspects of protection, resources, and methods that are classified or are sensitive. This is particularly true in the counterterrorism and intelligence arenas. Specific knowledge of the threat, the government's specific methods to deal with those threats, and technologies involved could compromise national security and intelligence collection methods. To protect the ability of those resources and methods to function safely and efficiently, they will not be included in this document.

Delimitations

It is beyond the scope of this thesis to analyze all of the interesting and applicable cases available for this study. The two selected case studies, coupled with a rigorous analysis of the doctrine and restraints, are adequate to highlight inconsistencies in the military's antiterrorism approach.

In practice, doctrine becomes a large volume of published works, and antiterrorism doctrine is no exception. Therefore, this study will only use those doctrinal documents specified for commanders or those that relate directly to the employment of forces (operations as opposed to engineering, law enforcement, etc.) and AT-specific writings. Review and analysis of the doctrinal aspects of antiterrorism will be limited to documents at the service and above levels. Regulations from subordinate commands will generally not be included in this study.

The practical application of antiterrorism programs at the lower levels of the doctrinal hierarchy spans a large envelope. It is beyond the scope of this study to analyze specific technical and procedural measures, such as the hardening of facilities or evaluating transportation routes for high-risk personnel. Instead, the analysis of the doctrine will simply divine the existence of that doctrine and demand its compliance with the DoD standard.

Significance of the Study

Strategic Setting. As described earlier, terrorism can have significant ramifications on the political and social well being of a country. Continued research and analysis are critical to protect the national interests of the U.S.

Operational Setting. Terrorism affects the DoD and members of the U.S. armed forces. In the past 25 years, terrorist attacks have killed over 300 DoD service members and civilians and injured more that 1,000. The loss in property and equipment has amounted to millions of dollars.[16] With increasing technology, terrorists can now acquire the capability to kill thousands of people in a very short period.

Tactical Setting. Individual members of the military have an inherent responsibility to assist in the protection of themselves, their families, DoD facilities, and material resources from terrorist attack. More encompassing, military commanders at every level have the duty to protect the troops in their command from these attacks. The decision by Secretary of Defense William Cohen not to promote the Air Force commander in charge of Khobar Towers at the time of the bombing, while controversial, is incontestable proof that senior leaders will hold commanders responsible for the effectiveness of their antiterrorist programs. A recurring subtheme throughout this document is to reiterate to commanders that it is their primary responsibility to provide protection for the members of their command.

In that light, it is imperative that commanders are provided the best doctrine possible. Only a continuous process of critically reviewing the doctrine, that which incorporates recommendations for improvement, will ensure American commanders have the necessary tools to successfully combat this critical threat.

The Research Topic

The subject of antiterrorism has gained heightened interest in the collective consciousness of the American public in the wake of the Murrah Federal Building in Oklahoma City and the attack on Khobar Towers in Saudi Arabia. All levels of government have placed emphasis on antiterrorism. The U.S. Congress has enacted new legislation at the request of the President (to whit, *The Antiterrorism and Effective Death Penalty Act of 1996*). Within the defense community, additional resources have been made available for this important facet of force protection. After the Khobar Towers attack, President Clinton asked for and received supplemental appropriations of $353 million for "various antiterrorism activities to increase physical security at overseas locations."[17]

Currently, the U.S. Special Operations Command, as designated lead agency for the DoD, is charged with reviewing and providing recommendations for improving the doctrinal basis for antiterrorism. This study, in consultation with the author's thesis committee chairman, evolved from a request for research from that command.

Assumptions

Since a review of the tactics, techniques, and procedures associated with the tactical applications of AT is beyond the scope of this study, it is assumed that improvements to the strategic and operational doctrine will have a "trickle-down" effect on the tactical doctrine.

This study also assumes that the applicable laws and presidential orders assigning lead agency responsibilities at the federal level will not change. Further, the assumption is that the understanding between the DoD and the DoS regarding the protection of military members overseas will not substantially change in the near future (more discussion about this topic later). Finally, regardless of the doctrine in place and prudent AT measures in force, a determined suicidal terrorist attack most probably will succeed. That said, even marginal improvement in the doctrine is worth seeking.

---

[1]While this particular group is fictitious, the U.S. Department of State lists thirty such international terrorist groups.

[2]Joint Staff, JP 3-07.2, *Joint Tactics, Techniques, and Procedures for Antiterrorism* (Washington, DC: DoD, 25 June 93), 8.

[3]U.S. Army, FM 100-5, *Operations* (Washington, DC: Department of the Army, June 1993), 6-7.

[4]Joint Staff, CJCSH 5260, *Commander's Handbook for Antiterrorism Readiness* (Washington, DC: DoD, 1 Jan 97), 1.

[5]FM 100-5, 6.

[6]FM 100-5, v.

[7]William J. Clinton, *A National Security Strategy for a New Century* (Washington, DC: The White House, May 1997), 5.

[8]Phillip Wilcox, *1996 Patterns of Global Terrorism Report* (Washington, DC: State Department, 1 May 1997), 1.

[9]Steven Presley, "Rise of Domestic Terrorism and Its Relation to United States Armed Forces" (Quantico, VA: Marine Corps Command and Staff College, 19 April 1996), Appendix E.

[10]Assistant Secretary of Defense for Special Operations and Low-Intensity Conflict, DoD Handbook 0-2000.12-H, *Protection of DoD Personnel and Activities Against Acts of Terrorism and Political Turbulence* (Washington, DC: DoD, 19 February 1993), xii.

[11]Joint Staff, JCS Publication 1-02, *DoD Dictionary* (Washington, DC: DoD, 23 March 1994), 219.

[12]Ibid., 109.

[13]Ibid., 44.

[14]Internal Security Act, Statutes at large 50, sec. 21, 797 (1950).

[15]DoD Handbook 0-2000.12-H, 4-3.

[16]General Wayne A. Downing, *Report of the Assessment of the Khobar Towers Bombing* (Washington, DC: Department of Defense, 30 August 1996), 5.

[17]William J. Clinton, "Statement on Counter-Terrorism Initiatives," *Weekly Compilation of Presidential Documents,* 16 September 1996, 1740.

CHAPTER 2

LITERATURE REVIEW

Terrorism has been the subject of countless works of literature, both in civilian writings and military studies. The majority of the relevant work in the field can be divided into three general categories: general history of terrorism, comprehending the threat of terrorism (which includes the psychology of terrorists), and specific antiterrorism (AT) writings. Additionally, published military writings in the form of regulations and manuals, augmented by informal handbooks, pamphlets and research papers, exist in quantity.

The publication medium is diverse and similarly prolific, encompassing scholarly writings, government reports from both the U.S. and other nations, specialized journals, military doctrine, and popular media. The Internet is gaining in popularity for both publicizing the terrorists' views and publishing AT works.

Background in Terrorism

Understanding the history of terrorism is an excellent beginning for the AT scholar. An excellent primer is Walter Laqueur's *Terrorism: A Study of National and International Violence*. Mr. Laqueur sets the stage for this study by charting the doctrine of terrorism itself. While the work is dated, it is still useful. Of significant relevance, Mr. Laqueur is one of the earliest writers to have recognized the terror potential of nuclear weapons, a growing concern in the world today. Currently, Mr. Laqueur is the Chairman of the International Research Council at the Center for Strategic and International Studies and is a prolific writer on all aspects of terrorism.

Ariel Merari compiles and edits the excellent book *On Terrorism and Combatting Terrorism* that chronicles the proceedings of one of the first big AT symposiums, the 1979 Tel-Aviv International Seminar. A key work in this compendium is Brian M. Jenkins' paper, "Terrorism-Prone Countries and Conditions." In this essay, Mr. Jenkins outlines several hypotheses explaining the root causes of terrorism, invaluable information to the AT body of knowledge. Again, this body is dated, and one hypothesis that reflects Communist ideology as a source of terrorism was, in hindsight, an oversimplification of the state sponsorship of terrorism.

Threat Literature

The U.S. State Department's annual publication *Patterns of Global Terrorism* (most current edition is 1996) is the definitive governmental report on the current status of terrorism activities and trends worldwide. Mandated by public law, this report is extremely useful, albeit with decided shortcomings. Foremost among these is the lack of data on terrorism that occurs in a domestic venue, such as the significant internal carnage in Algeria.

Domestically, the National Security Division of the Federal Bureau of Investigation produces specialized reports on combatting terrorism. One such report issued for the 1996 Atlanta Olympics, *The Militia Movement* outlines the growing phenomenon of right-wing terrorism in the U.S. This type of information is very important to military commanders; for example one particular group uses identification cards that are remarkably similar to the Geneva Conventions Identification Card issued by the Department of Defense (DoD). Their report, *53rd Presidential Inauguration Threat Assessment* is a brief but insightful look into the intelligence functions of the nation's lead agency for combatting domestic terrorism.

The potential proliferation of weapons of mass destruction has had particular appeal in the popular media recently. The *Wall Street Journal* in December 1997 reported on Secretary of Defense Cohen's dramatic display on national television of the implications of a biological attack on Washington, DC, with a quantity of anthrax roughly the size of a five- pound sack of sugar. The AT implications are twofold. First, such reporting heightens the public's (and military members') awareness of terrorism. This is positive in the sense it brings attention to needed funding and operational issues. Second, it confuses the doctrinal issues with emotion and political posturing. The negative connotations are that plays on emotion may unduly influence doctrinal reform.

15

Antiterrorism-specific Literature

Dr. Karl A. Seger's *The Antiterrorism Handbook* presents an AT prescription for individuals and corporations in a genre designed to commercialize and sell AT protection to those at risk. While written in a hypothetical-scenario style that is more akin to a novel, Dr. Seger presents an excellent discussion of interagency cooperation in an AT-specific forum. In that regard, this book overcomes the attempt to commercialize AT.

The United States General Accounting Office (GAO) offers the most critical review of the current Defense Department's AT efforts in its contemporary report *Combatting Terrorism: Status of DoD Efforts to Protect Its Forces Overseas*. In its approach, the GAO outlines the AT actions DoD elements have taken and those that remain to be accomplished. While conceding numerous specific efforts have been implemented, much work remains to be done, particularly in the doctrinal area.

Lieutenant Colonel Dale Pangman (U.S.A.F.) wrote a Naval War College paper titled "Can the U.S. Adequately Protect its Forces?" in which he argues convincingly that the U.S. military must do more to make American forces less vulnerable to attack. His work includes recommendations for intelligence fusion cells, increased interservice and international cooperation, and change deployment patterns to an expeditionary concept.

The March 1996 Congressional testimony of the Honorable Morris D. Busby (U.S. State Department's Coordinator for Counterterrorism, 1989-1991) identifies three problems with the current U.S. AT structure: sharing information between intelligence and law enforcement, collecting information on groups operating in the United States, and conducting interagency operations. The latter problem is a major finding of this study.

The Honorable H. Allen Holmes, Assistant Secretary of Defense (Special Operations and Low Intensity Conflict) is interviewed in "Countering Terrorist Challenges" in the February 1998 edition of *Armed Forces Journal*. He presents a state-of-the-union-style address that touches upon all the combatting terrorism efforts currently underway within the DoD.

The recurring *Security Awareness Bulletin* from the DoD Security Institute is an excellent source of current AT thinking. Lynn Fischer presents her view that terrorism is everyone's concern in "Antiterrorism Awareness: Changing the Mindset." She implicitly endorses the contention that AT must operate across the entire spectrum of military operations with the statement, "Both policy and common sense dictate that general AT awareness be a standard element in security indoctrination for Department of Defense personnel."[1]

Military Doctrine

This work primarily consists of comparing and contrasting the official military antiterrorism doctrine. Chapters 3 and 4 give a complete review and analysis of the official AT doctrine currently in force.

The monograph "What is Doctrine? An Overview of United States Military Doctrine" produced by the Joint Team at the U.S. Army Command and General Staff College, Fort Leavenworth Kansas, and "The Joint Doctrine Story" produced by the Joint Staff, Washington, DC, were indispensable for establishing the hierarchy and the theoretical roles of doctrine within the U.S. military structure and should be read before evaluating this study.

Case Studies

The author has attempted to anchor each case study by a significant government report when available, accompanied by ancillary governmental reports, documents, and journalistic accounts.

The definitive governmental work on the bombing of the Beirut barracks is *the Report of the DoD Commission on Beirut International Airport Terrorist Act, October 23, 1983*. This report is commonly referred to as the "Long Commission Report" after the chairman of the commission, retired Admiral Robert L. J. Long. Commissioned by the Secretary of Defense on 7

November 1983, the investigation was charged "to conduct a thorough and independent inquiry into all facets and circumstances surrounding the 23 October 1983 terrorist attack on the Marine Battalion Landing Team (BLT) Headquarters at the Beirut International Airport."[2]

Three days after the Khobar Towers attack, the Secretary of Defense chartered an assessment of the "facts and circumstances surrounding the tragedy . . . a fast, unvarnished and independent look at what happened there and offer ideas on how we can try to prevent such a tragedy in the future."[3] This assessment task force, led by retired General Wayne A. Downing (U.S. Army) produced the core document, *Report of the Assessment of the Khobar Towers Bombing*, which anchored the Secretary of Defense's report to the President. Both documents demand considerable scrutiny, as these provide an outstanding sense of what is expected in a doctrinal sense.

Returning to Lieutenant Colonel Pangman's Naval War College paper discussed above, he also includes a section that compares and contrasts the two case studies. His analysis, while used to support a different thesis, is an insightful piece that parallels some of the conclusions of this study.

In summary, the literature review for this project shows a considerable historical and contemporary interest in all aspects of antiterrorism. The depth and breadth is sufficient to identify the problems inherent in AT as well as the desired end state of AT efforts. The thesis can now turn to an extensive evaluation of the doctrine in the remainder of this paper.

---

[1]Lynn F. Fischer, "Antiterrorism Awareness: Changing the Mindset," *Security Awareness Bulletin* (Washington, DC: DoD Security Institute, March 96), 1.

[2]Admiral Robert L. J. Long, *Report of the DoD Commission on Beirut International Airport Terrorist Act* (Washington, DC: DoD, 20 December 1983), 19.

[3]William Perry, *Report to the President and the Congress--The Protection of U.S. Forces Deployed Abroad* (Washington, DC: DoD, 15 September 1996), 5.

CHAPTER 3

RESEARCH METHODOLOGY

Doctrine Defined?

How is doctrine defined and what are its prominent characteristics? The Department of Defense (DoD) defines military doctrine as "fundamental principles by which the military forces or elements thereof guide their actions in support of national objectives. It is authoritative but requires judgment in application."[1] This definition can be divided into two simple elements, the function of providing fundamental principles and the characteristic that it is directive in nature but must tempered with judgement.

Before proceeding deeper into the discussion about doctrine, it is important to note that not all the military services subscribe to that definition. It is instructional to view how each military service promulgates a different view of doctrine; this information has been captured in table 1. To summarize the variations, each service agrees that the application of doctrine must be tempered with judgment but considerable disagreement exists as to the authoritative (sometimes referred to as directive) nature of the doctrine promulgated.

The implications of this condition on this study are significant. With five different views on the nature of doctrine present in today's military (albeit varying considerably in degree of divergence), it must be argued that military members from the different services will look at the antiterrorism (AT) doctrine from a different perspective and with a different concept of compliance with the doctrine.

This condition is analogous to a football game where the joint force commander (the coach) is conducting the game under National Football League rules while the various players are using Canadian rules, Australian league standards, and English rugby rules simultaneously. Therefore, as a matter of practical consideration, the first step in AT doctrinal reform is for the services to abide by a common definition of doctrine!

Table 1. Definition of Doctrine by Service

Service	Definition of Doctrine	
	Declaration of Authoritative or Directive	Judgment Required?
U.S. Air Force	"A statement of officially sanctioned beliefs and warfighting principles, which describe and guide the proper use of air and space forces in military operations. In application, doctrine must be treated with judgement."	Y
	"It is authoritative but not directive."	
U.S. Army	"Fundamental principles by which military forces or elements thereof guide their actions in support of national objectives."	Y
	"It is authoritative but requires judgement in application."	
U.S. Navy	"Doctrine is the starting point from which we develop solutions and options to address the specific warfighting demands and challenges we face in conducting operations other than war. To be useful, doctrine must be uniformly known and understood. With doctrine we gain standardization, without relinquishing freedom of judgment and the commander's need to exercise initiative in battle."	Y
	"Doctrine is conceptual--a shared way of thinking that is not directive."	
U.S. Marine Corps	"Doctrine is a teaching of the fundamental beliefs of the Marine Corps on the subject of war, from its nature and theory to its preparation and conduct. Doctrine establishes a particular way of thinking about war and a way of fighting . . . In short, it establishes the way we practice our profession."	Y
	"Our doctrine does not consist of procedures to be applied in specific situations so much as it sets forth general guidance that requires judgment in application. Therefore, while authoritative, doctrine is not prescriptive."	

Sources: U.S.A.F.: AFDD 1, *Air Force Basic Doctrine*, (Washington, DC: Department of the Air Force, September 1997), 1; U.S.A.: FM 101-5-1, *Operational Terms and Graphics*, (Washington, DC: Department of the Army, 30 September 1997), 1-55; U.S.N.: NDP 1, *Naval Warfare*, (Washington, DC: Department of the Navy, 18 March 1994), I; and U.S.M.C.: MCDP 1, *Warfighting*, (Washington, DC: Department of the Navy, 20 June 1997), 35.

The Analytical Tree: Structure Plus Content

The analysis of the doctrine requires a method to judge the validity of the AT doctrinal structure as well as the content itself. An excellent departure point to synthesize such a model is Colonel Dennis Drew's anatomy of doctrine.[2] Colonel Drew is a noted U.S. Air Force expert in the field of doctrine and airpower theory. Colonel Drew wrote "On Trees and Leaves; A New View of Doctrine" to highlight the shortfalls in Air Force doctrine in the early 1980s. Specifically, Colonel Drew recognized the existence of a hierarchy of doctrine: fundamental, environmental, and organizational writings that when linked together provide the structure of doctrine. He chose the metaphor of a tree to represent this construct

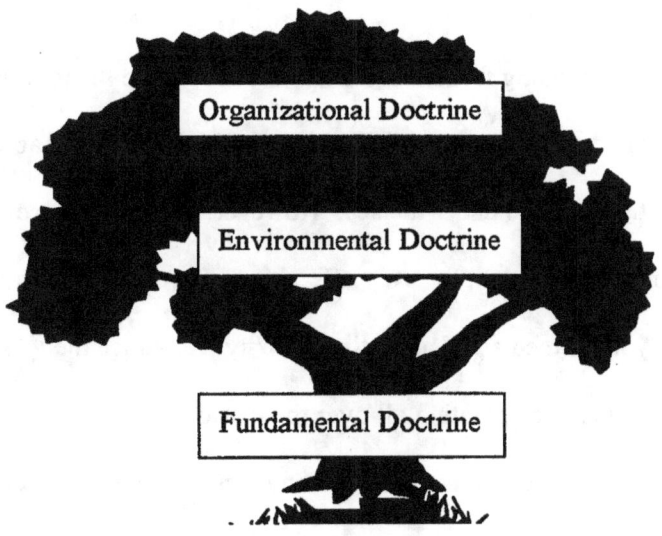

Figure 1. Drew's Tree

(see figure 1). This model has an intrinsic, familiar appeal to the author for current Air Force doctrine follows this construction.

According to Drew's model, the doctrine placed in the fundamental category should contain certain characteristics: an assertion about the basic beliefs concerning the history and nature of the war against terrorism (i.e., what national interests are at stake), possess a "timeless" quality based on basic concepts, and be relatively exempt from rapidly changing

21

political leanings or specific technological advances that would render it obsolete. The national guidance and the DoD writings will form the basis of the fundamental doctrinal structure. Tabulated, the criterion appears in table 2.

Table 2. Fundamental Structure Criteria

Basic Beliefs: History and nature of terrorism.
Timelessness: Basic concepts hold true across time (implicitly or explicitly)
Not invalidated by changing politics or technological advances

Environmental doctrine describes the ability of the military to successfully conduct its business in the anticipated environment. According to Drew, environmental doctrine is narrower and more focused than fundamental doctrine and should provide more specific guidance to the commander.

Before proceeding further, it is important to define the term environment. In Drew's model, an example of environmental doctrine would describe the ability of the Navy to conduct operations on and under the sea. However, in the context of this study, physical boundaries must be irrelevant for truly effective antiterrorist doctrine must exist simultaneously in all media and at all times. Why? Because the U.S. military continually has forces deployed and operating all over the world.

It is also necessary to consider the environment in the context of the spectrum of conflict. Today and for the foreseeable future, military operations are generally expected to operate across a large spectrum of involvement, ranging from a single person to the massed forces required for a major regional conflict, and at all levels of violence. This spectrum can range from peaceful low-level assistance supporting civil authorities to fighting a global war.

By Drew's definition, the value of environmental doctrine lies in its adaptability; it may change more rapidly than fundamental doctrine for it allows for technological advances without becoming invalid. The last thing the analysis must show is that the doctrine considers emerging technologies and advocates incorporating beneficial changes that exploits those technologies.

The summary of the environmental structure criteria is depicted in table 3. The environmental doctrinal structure can be judged as adequate if it requires the doctrine to function at all times and in all conditions. The structure must account for spanning the entire spectrum of activities ranging from unilateral training on a local training range in the United States through humanitarian operations in a disaster-ravaged country in Southeast Asia to a major regional conflict in Korea. Further, the doctrine must acknowledge the need to incorporate the rapidly changing technological advances of today.

Table 3. Environment Structure Criteria

Worldwide applicability in all mediums at all times
Covers entire spectrum of operations and all levels of violence
Acknowledges the need to incorporate emerging technologies

Drew's last category is organizational doctrine. This is the melding of abstract fundamental and changing environmental doctrine into relevant, narrowly focused guidance. Organizational doctrine must provide particular forces (U.S. Army troops) in a particular environment (force projection operations) at a particular time (on a deployment) with specific courses of action relevant to the threat. As previously mentioned, it is beyond the scope of this study to explicitly analyze this level of doctrine. It is sufficient to recognizing its existence (or lack thereof).

Table 4. Organizational Structure Criteria

Acknowledged existence

Drew's model is therefore capable of describing the structure of the fundamental, environmental, and organizational doctrine. Omission of any of the criteria would be an indication that change is needed. But alone it is not quite sufficient. Taking this construction one step farther, this study will take his structural model and merge it with a strategic-operational-tactical view of the content of the doctrine. The benefit of this hybrid model is its ability to link higher-level with lower-level doctrine. This will allow incongruities to be readily apparent.

To evaluate the content of the strategic doctrine (the same writings as in the fundamental case) a good tool is the strategy equation articulated by Colonel Arthur F. Lykke, Jr., in his paper "Toward an Understanding of Military Strategy"[3] which is taught at the Army's Command and General Staff College. That equation is:

$$Strategy = Ends + Ways + Means$$

In this context, the strategic doctrine should identify three components. First, the doctrine should articulate the *ends* in view with regard to AT efforts. In other words, what are the national AT objectives? Second, the doctrine should specify the various *ways* or the programs designed to accomplish the objectives. Third, the doctrine must identify the *means* or the resources (money, materiel, manpower, etc.) required to meet the objective. The study will simultaneously evaluate the fundamental and strategic criteria of the doctrine. Table 5 shows the criteria for valid strategic content.

Table 5. Strategic Content Criteria

Ends Identified (objective)
Ways Identified (programs)
Means Identified (resources)

The operational doctrine should provide the linkage between the strategic and the tactical and be geared towards the senior field commanders. In order to gauge whether the operational content is sufficient to bridge the two, the doctrine must acknowledge the multifaceted aspect in the way U.S. military forces are organized. First, the military services (Army, Navy, Air Force, and Marine Corps) conduct unilateral operations and maintain installations worldwide and therefore have AT responsibilities in that context. Second, they also organize, train, and equip forces for use by joint forces commanders (U.S. Central Command, U.S. Pacific Command, etc.) in the manner General Schwarzkopf commanded all U.S. and coalition troops in Desert Storm. In that circumstance, both the services and the joint force commander have AT roles and responsibilities. Third, commanders must orchestrate their activities with agencies and organizations outside of the Department of Defense. In applying the AT doctrine, the DoD often plays a supporting role to other civilian organizations, therefore there must be a methodology to both provide and receive support from those outside agencies. Finally, American forces are expected to operate as part of multinational coalitions. Again, there must be an adequate doctrinal base for use in a multinational environment. This criterion is shown in table 6. The operational writings are the same as those in the environmental category and will be analyzed at the same time.

Table 6. Operational Content Criteria

Unilateral employment
Joint employment
Interagency agreements
Multinational considerations

The tactical doctrine should contain the tactics, techniques and procedures (TTPs) used daily by lower echelon commanders to win the individual antiterrorism battles. Again, this study will not specifically analyze the details of this level of doctrine, but will accept as adequate joint or service doctrine whose TTPs are the same as or more restrictive than those in the DoD 0-2000.12-H, the current Department of Defense standard. An evaluation of this category will accompany the analysis of the organizational doctrine and the resulted presented according to table 7.

Table 7. Tactical Content Criteria

TTPs meet DoD standards

Three other items remain out of sight but are nonetheless critical to the health of the metaphorical tree: the roots, the soil, and the sap. Owing to the probability that American forces will operate in the joint and multinational environment, the analysis of these three aspects of doctrine will be limited to the operational-level DoD and joint publications.

The Roots: Intelligence versus the Threat

AT doctrine is figuratively rooted in the intelligence capability of commanders to identify the threat arrayed against them. While it may seem obvious, the doctrine must coherently identify the current terrorist threat. As the ancient Chinese general Sun Tzu said, "If you know yourself and you know your enemy, in one hundred battles you will never be in peril."[4]

As such, intelligence has been described as the *sine qua non* of AT. Intelligence is the military function of synthesizing "information and knowledge about an adversary obtained through observation, investigation, analysis, or understanding."[5] Historically, the generation of adequate intelligence conducive to AT efforts has fell short of the mark. In testifying before Congress, Ambassador Busby indicated that two of the three major problems facing the U.S. in regards to current antiterrorism efforts dealt with the generation and sharing of critical intelligence.[6] In order to demonstrate the proper doctrinal foundation for the AT intelligence effort, the doctrine must show cognizance of the current and anticipated threat.

The Soil: Capabilities and Restrictions

Commanders inherently have certain authority granted to them to employ forces to accomplish a given mission. By extension, commanders have vested authority to conduct AT activities, "the inherent responsibility of commanders to protect the military installations, equipment, or personnel under their command."[7] But what happens when the commander desires to take a particular action but is without the necessary authority to implement that action? There are various laws, regulations, and agreements that limit the ability of commanders to act. While a full discussion of this topic will take place in the next chapter, it is sufficient at this point to recognize that a commander's authority is limited. Therefore, there must be a mechanism to request and receive the requisite authority.

Additionally, the law of diminishing returns indicates that a commander will reach a point when the ability to accomplish the assigned mission, the *raison d'être* of military organizations, is jeopardized by the AT precautions being implemented. The commander will simply run out of resources or the measures being implemented will be counterproductive and self-defeating with respect to the mission. Identifying and understanding the most important of these limiting factors must be part of the doctrine writers' toolbox.

The Sap: The Concept of Security

The sap or lifeblood of this tree is embodied in the concept of security. It must flow throughout the tree, providing nourishment to every part. In chapter 1, antiterrorism was expressed as a subset of force protection. In turn, force protection can be said to fall under the concept of *security*, again defined by the DoD as "measures taken by a military unit, an activity or installation to protect itself against all acts designed to, or which may, impair its effectiveness."[8] On an even larger scale, *security* is itself one of the fundamental principles of war embodied in American military theory,

> The purpose of security is to never permit the enemy to acquire unexpected advantage. Security enhances freedom of action by reducing friendly vulnerability to hostile acts, influence, or surprise. Security results from the measures taken by command errors to protect their forces. Staff planning and an understanding of enemy strategy, tactics, and doctrine will enhance security. Risk is inherent in military operations. Application of this principle includes prudent risk management, not undue caution. Protecting the force increases friendly combat power and preserves freedom of action.[9]

The "principles of war" is a military concept that can trace its roots to antiquity, and the need to embody *security* as one of those principles has always been significant. Sun Tzu wrote, "If I am able to determine the enemy dispositions while at the same time I conceal my own then I can concentrate and he must divide."[10] Napoleon included a similar view of security in his Maxim II, "In forming the plan of a campaign, it is requisite to foresee everything the enemy may do, and to be prepared with the necessary means to counteract it."[11]

More recently, the military writer Jomini implicitly included the concept of security as part of his fundamental principle of war, describing it, "In carrying by strategic combinations the mass of the forces of an army successively upon the decisive points of a theatre of war, and as much as possible upon the communications of the enemy, without endangering its own.[12]

In light of this obvious importance of the principle of security, it is the best representative indicator that the operational doctrine is valid. Therefore, the concept of security, force protection, and antiterrorism must be explicitly stated in each of the designated publications at the operational level.

In summary, there are three additional, distinct common criterions implicitly necessary when analyzing the validity of the DoD and joint AT doctrine. They are: an intelligence structure capable of identifying the threat that spans the operational continuum, a method for overcoming the impediments to implement required actions, and an identification of *security, force protection,* and *antiterrorism* as necessary in all operations.

When all the criteria developed thus far are placed together, a clear picture emerges as to the visible composition of the doctrinal tree. The fundamental structure and the strategic content comprise the trunk. The environmental and operational counterparts constitute the branches. The organizational and tactical writings represent the leaves. The criteria are summarized in table 8. When placed against the specific documents and analyzed in the next chapter, a plus (+) will indicate acceptance and a minus (-) will connote failure to meet the specific criterion. Although not visible, the tree is rooted in intelligence, grown in the soil of capabilities and restrictions, and fed with security, therefore these subjects also need to be discussed.

Table 8 Consolidated Criteria

Fundamental
Basic Beliefs: History and Nature of Terrorism
Timelessness: Basic concepts hold true across time (demonstrated or stated)
Not invalidated by changing politics or technological advances
Strategic
Ends Identified (objective)
Ways Identified (programs)
Means Identified (resources)
Environmental
Worldwide applicability in all mediums at all times
Covers entire spectrum of operations and all levels of violence
Acknowledges the need to incorporate emerging technologies
Operational
Unilateral employment
Joint employment
Interagency agreements
Multinational considerations
Organizational
Acknowledged existence
Tactical
TTPs meet DoD standards

Case Study Approach

Now with a robust approach to evaluating the doctrinal structure and content, complete with restrictions and constraints, it is necessary to construct an analogous method to evaluate the case studies. This problem of analyzing experiences to develop a series of lessons learned logically lends itself to the case study approach of historical examples. Two cases separated by thirteen years have been selected for their remarkable similarities in both the types of attack and the ramifications after the fact. A simple method of comparing and contrasting the common features of the case studies against the current joint doctrine will

highlight key points for refinement into proposed doctrinal changes.

---

[1]JP 1-02, 175.

[2]Dennis Drew, "Of Trees and Leaves: A New View of Doctrine." *Air University Review,* (Jan-Feb 1982), 40-49.

[3]Colonel Arthur F. Lykke, Jr., "Toward an Understanding of Military Strategy." *Military Strategy: Theory and Application,* in *DJCO Selected Readings Book: Fundamentals of Operational Warfighting I (Module 1),* (Fort Leavenworth, Kansas: U.S. Army Command and General Staff College, 1997), 1-E-1 thru 1-E-2.

[4]Sun Tzu, *The Art of War,* tran. by Samuel B. Griffith, (New York: Oxford University Press, 1971), 98.

[5]JP 1-02, 268.

[6]Honorable Morris D. Busby in testimony before the United States Senate Permanent Subcommittee on Investigations Committee on Governmental Affairs, 27 March 1996. [transcript on-line]; available from http://www.counterterrorism.com/busby.htm; Internet; accessed 10 March 1998.

[7]CJCSH 5260, 7.

[8]JP 1-02, 473.

[9]Joint Staff, Joint Publication 3-0, *Doctrine for Joint Operations* (Washington, DC: DoD, 1 February 1995), A-2.

[10]Sun Tzu, 98.

[11]Napoleon I, *The Military Maxims of Napoleon,* ed. by David Chandler (New York: Macmillan, 1988), 6.

[12]Baron Antoine-Henri Jomini, *Principal Combinations of Strategy, of Grand Tactics, and of Military Policy* (New York: G.P. Putnam and Company, 1854), 80, *in The Evolution of Modern Warfare Term I Book of Readings* (Fort Leavenworth, KS: Combat Studies Institute, U.S. Army Command and General Staff College, 1997), 255.

CHAPTER 4

ANALYSIS: HOW HEALTHY IS THE TREE?

> "Still it is the task of military science in an age of peace to prevent the doctrines from being too badly wrong."[1]
>
> Michael Howard, "Military Science in an Age of Peace"

The Current Doctrine

The analysis begins with the consideration of the current doctrine using the methodology developed in the previous chapter. In that context, a detailed examination of the fundamental doctrine, the environmental doctrine, and the organizational doctrine of current U.S. AT programs will be made. Depicted graphically, the hierarchical representation of that doctrine would look like the model shown in figure 2.

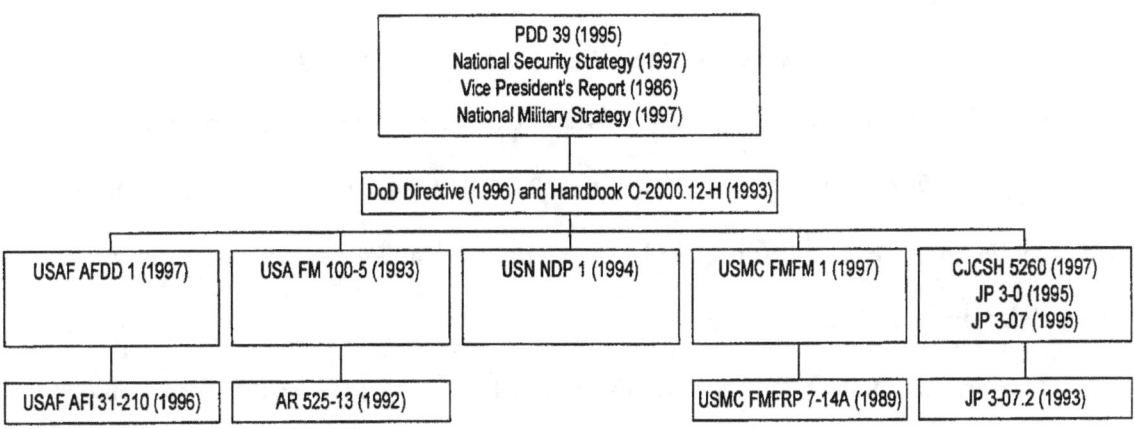

Figure 2. Doctrinal Hierarchy

The top block designates the fundamental/strategic level, the middle two levels represent the environmental/operational, and the lowest level specifies the organizational/tactical doctrine. While some would argue that the national-level doctrine is not doctrine at all but a statement of national policy, it is incumbent to view these writings as the expression of the President's (an thus the commander's) intent, a concept firmly embedded in military doctrine. Therefore, it certainly has a home in this study.

The environment and operational Department of Defense (DoD) writings occupy a different level not to imply a separate category but to reflect their position of ascendancy over the service and joint doctrine. The DoD writings are proclaimed by the Secretary of Defense as being directive in nature with respect to all DoD personnel and facilities. The service-specific instructions are only applicable to members of the particular service (i.e., an Army regulation would not be binding on an Air Force commander in a unilateral setting). The joint publications are applicable in the joint environment, at which point they assume precedence over the service regulations. All told, this structure can create schizophrenia where joint force commanders are assigned subordinates from different services that normally operate under different rules. This condition, much like the problem reaching a military-wide definition of doctrine, must be resolved!

The Trunk: Fundamental and Strategic Doctrine

Thus, the *Presidential Decision Directive (PDD) 39, A National Security Strategy for A New Century*, the *Vice President's Report*, and the *National Military Strategy* are considered as constituting the fundamental doctrine. With the exception of the *Vice President's Report*, they are considered directive in nature.

It is now important to determine if this body of literature addresses the three requirements necessary for Drew's model. To reiterate the criteria, the doctrine must first provide some basic beliefs about the nature of the war against terrorism. Second, the doctrine cannot be time-sensitive; it must be of an enduring nature. Third, the writings must account for technology but not be invalidated by it.

In order to demonstrate the first criterion, the doctrine must show that the national security of the U.S., and by extension the armed forces, is continually threatened by terrorism. The second criterion can be proven implicitly by a lack of change in the policy or explicitly by announcing a set duration for the doctrine. The third criterion must be explicitly accounted for; technology is changing too rapidly to rely on implication or inference.

The study begins to address these questions by using *PDD 39* as the capstone for the simple reason it is the ultimate expression of the President of the United States. It is readily apparent he sets the proper stage by stating in the introduction:

> It is the policy of the United States to deter, defeat and respond vigorously to all terrorist attacks on our territory and against our citizens, or facilities, whether they occur domestically, in international waters or airspace or on foreign territory. The United States regards all such terrorism as a *potential threat to national security* [emphasis mine] as well as a criminal act and will apply all appropriate means to combat it. In doing so, the U.S. shall pursue vigorously effort to deter and preempt, apprehend and prosecute, or assist other governments to prosecute, individuals who perpetrate or plan to perpetrate such attacks.[2]

By any measure, this certainly describes the national policy in no uncertain terms. Note the prominent inclusion of the words like "deter" and "defeat" that set the stage for the antiterrorism aspects of the collective war against terrorism. One can infer that by presenting "Reducing our Vulnerabilities" as the first paragraph in the document, the President sets top priority for the AT aspects of the document. *PDD 39* has been shown to meet the first criterion.

The *National Security Strategy* also explicitly designates terrorism as a threat to U.S. national interests. In describing the three groups of threats (regional or state-centered, transnational, and threats from weapons of mass destruction) terrorism is specified in two and implied in the third (regional or state centered). As, with *PDD 39*, the *National Security Strategy* has been shown to meet the first criterion.

The *Vice President's Report* of 1986 provides the historical basis and is still referenced in all the subordinate literature. It has a section devoted to the nature of terrorism. It likewise characterizes terrorism directed against the U.S. as a "potential threat to its national security"[3] and emphasizes prevention of terrorist attacks, "Dealing effectively with terrorism requires long-term measures for providing physical and personal security, training personnel, and enlisting the

33

cooperation of other governments in protective measures, in gathering and sharing intelligence and in the elimination of terrorist threats."[4]

Turning to the last document in this category, the Chairman of the Joint Chiefs of Staff (CJCS) in authoring the *National Military Strategy* not surprisingly mimics the *National Security Strategy* in calling terrorism a threat to U.S. national interests. It also places an emphasis on the threat of terrorism: "there are states and other actors who can challenge us and our allies conventionally and by asymmetric means such as terrorism."[5] Further, places this threat in a continuum, "beginning at home . . . from predeployment through employment and redeployment."[6] Certainly this is a good measure of the nature of the problem.

The comparison of these documents over time, using the *Vice President's Report* as a baseline, shows that although separated by over a decade all the documents align closely in spirit if not necessarily in the letter of the writings. While both the *PDD 39* (and similar instruments differently named) and the *National Security Strategy* are published by the incumbent President, they are naturally subject to change with the inauguration of a new administration. In a display of continuity of American policy, the previous editions of these documents show the substance has in fact changed very little with differing presidential administrations. This certainly demonstrates an enduring quality in articulating American national interests. To further illustrate this point, while the *Vice President's Report* was published by a Republican administration and the current *PDD 39* and the *National Security Strategy* were published by a Democratic administration, they are quite complimentary and there is no trace of political leanings or partisan acrimony. In fact, the *Vice President's Report* states succinctly, "Terrorism is a bipartisan issue and one that members of Congress have jointly and judiciously addressed in recent years."[7] Clearly, this is one area of national interest that is devoid of partisan politics and has endured the test of time. The *National Military Strategy* explicitly sets its strategic direction on a course to last for the next five years. The second fundamental criterion of timelessness has been met.

Having collectively described the effect of the problem in terms of national interests and the enduring quality of the doctrine adequately, the last element must now be examined. To satisfy the final criterion, specific technological advances must not invalidate the doctrine. Without argument, great technological advances have taken place in the period since the *Vice President's Report* was published. At that time, the Internet was only known to a small group of scientists and physicists. Today, one can discover volumes of information about terrorism itself on the World Wide Web. Other evolutionary and revolutionary technologies have progressed similarly. All the documents in the fundamental category encourage the participants in the fight against terrorism to engage in a robust program of research and development to foster technological advances in the AT fight. That said, none (correctly) base their foundations on any particular technology. The *National Security Strategy* addresses this issue by saying, "This strategy took into account the revolution in technology that not only enriches our lives, but makes it possible for terrorists, criminals and drug traffickers to challenge the safety of our citizens and the security of our borders in new ways."[8] Perhaps the best representation of the role of technology is articulated in the *National Military Strategy*. It charges the military to embrace technology but simultaneously warns us against accepting it in toto: "As we reshape our forces to meet the challenges of a changing world, we will leverage emerging technologies to enhance the capabilities of our servicemen and women through development of new doctrine, organizations, material, and training. . . . However, they are not a panacea. We must recognize that each includes inherent vulnerabilities; each must be applicable across the range of operations; and each must enhance the human capability of our forces."[9]

According to Drew's model, these words from the CJCS set the correct conditions for specific resolution of technological issues at the next level of doctrine--precisely where it should be.

In summary, the fundamental doctrine appears to be sound based upon the three-part criteria: descriptive of the fundamental nature of terrorism, valid over long periods of time, and free from changes attributable to political leanings or specific technological advances. Now it is time to discover to its merits as strategic doctrine.

The strategic level of doctrine is that which is necessary to identify national security objectives (ends), develop AT programs (ways) and use national resources (means). To measure the first criterion, all the documents have been shown (in developing the basic beliefs argument above) to explicitly name the prevention of terrorist attacks against U.S. interests as a national security objective.

PDD 39 says, "The United States shall reduce its vulnerabilities to terrorism, at home and abroad."[10] In applying the policy specifically to the responsibilities of the DoD in the antiterrorism role, the document directs that the Secretary of Defense "shall reduce vulnerabilities affecting the security of all U.S. military personnel (except those assigned to diplomatic missions) and facilities."[11] Clearly the emphasis is placed on establishing and improving antiterrorism capabilities.

The *National Security Strategy* is also an expression of the President's guidance to the United States military establishment. References to terrorism abound throughout the document, and the objective with regard to antiterrorism is well expressed as "[U.S.] approaches are meant to prevent, disrupt, and defeat terrorist operations before they occur."[12]

As the *Vice President's Report* was crafted in an era when the emphasis was on responding to terrorism rather than preventing it, little is documented in regard to a preventative objective. It does outline the U.S. policy to "act in concert with other nations or unilaterally when necessary to *prevent* [emphasis mine] or respond to terrorist acts."[13] While not expansive, it is unequivocal.

One would expect the *National Military Strategy*, as a lower level of guidance, to provide

a less-generic, more specific end state, and the researcher is not disappointed. To describe that

end state, the CJCS used the encompassing term "force protection" and said this about the way

the future should look: "Multiple layers of protection for U.S. forces and facilities at all levels,

beginning at home, enable U.S. forces to maintain freedom of action from predeployment through

employment and redeployment. Fluid battlefields and the potential ability of adversaries to

orchestrate asymmetric threats against our forces require that we seek every means to protect our

forces. Comprehensive force protection requires the employment of a full array of active and

passive measures . . . Force protection initiatives must thus address all aspects of potential threats,

to include terrorism."[14]

Therefore, the doctrine has met the first strategic content criterion, an identifiable end

state. The summary table will reflect this finding accordingly.

The doctrine must now demonstrate it has the means to identify the ways to reach the end

state. *PDD 39* does little more than implement a programmatic methodology by designating lead

agencies with specific AT responsibilities. The *National Security Strategy* identifies various

instruments of national power that can be brought to bear: diplomatic initiatives with other

countries, intelligence cooperation, law enforcement efforts, and economic activities. Specific

programs include bolstering aviation security, improving protection for American transportation

systems, and increasing AT measures for overseas personnel.

While the *Vice President's Report* has an extensive repertoire of proposals for programs,

initiatives, and activities, most have long been implemented or rendered obsolete by changing

circumstances in the twelve years since the report was published.

The *National Military Strategy* uses two of the three elements of the conceptual strategy

of "Shape, Respond, and Prepare" to implicitly identify strategic ways. Military forces are to

shape their AT environment by inherent deterrence qualities (physical protection measures, threat

37

of deadly force, etc.). The military is directed to prepare for an uncertain future with sufficient capabilities and infrastructure to accomplish the entire spectrum of military operations, including AT activities.

In addressing the ability of the doctrine to identify the means for conducting antiterrorism, the guidance does little more than identifying the DoD responsibilities necessary for successful antiterrorism efforts and directs that adequate resources be applied to the problem. The implication is that the inherent capabilities of the various military services and the joint command structure are the national resources in the AT battle. As for specific funding, *PDD 39* directs that each agency "shall bear the costs"[15] which can be construed to mean the DoD should include AT factors in its budget submission. The *National Security Strategy* states that the "Administration is also working with Congress in increase the ability . . . to combat terrorism through augmented funding and manpower."[16] The *National Military Strategy* does not direct the application of specific military resources to AT efforts. The *Vice President's Report* is irrelevant as it is not directive in nature. In reporting on the current status of the allocation of resources, a report in the *Kansas City Star* recently said, "Despite authorities' enhanced efforts, America is still underprepared, according to a series of reports from the General Accounting Office. One report, which examined government spending on terrorism programs, concluded that 'because governmentwide priorities for combating terrorism have not been established, there is no basis to have reasonable assurance that the highest priority requirements are being met.'"[17]

In the absence of specific allocation of resources, the strategic content criterion of identifiable means has not been met.

All told, the doctrine has mixed scores in response to the scrutiny required to prove fundamental and strategic worth. Collectively, this subset of the AT doctrine has been proven to contain clear beliefs about the nature of the conflict, is timeless, apolitical and not rendered obsolete by new technologies. Strategically, the doctrine for the most part consistently identifies the national security objectives. However, the treatment of ways and means shows considerable gaps and must be corrected.

The findings are summarized in table 9. The trunk of Drew's doctrinal tree is not well and some prescriptive medicine is in order. Foremost is the need to specify at the national level what the AT priorities are. Even if AT programs are funded, prioritization should direct where the money can used with the most efficiency. Additional resources are being sought, "with the White House asking for a record $6.7 billion to fight terrorism."[18] But only sound leadership at the highest levels coupled with congressional action can help heal the trunk of the tree.

Table 9. Fundamental/Strategic Score Card

	PDD 39	NSS	VPR	NMS
Fundamental Structure Criteria				
Basic Beliefs: History and nature of terrorism	+	+	+	+
Timelessness	+	+	+	+
Not invalidated by politics or technology	+	+	+	+
Strategic Content Criteria				
Ends Identified	+	+	-	+
Ways Identified	-	+	-	+
Means Identified	-	-	-	-

The Branches: Environmental and Operational Doctrine

Turning attention to the environmental and operational doctrine; that which is defined as the DoD Directive 2000.12, *DoD Combating Terrorism Program* and its accompanying handbook DoD 0-2000.12-H, *Protection of DoD Personnel and Activities Against Acts of Terrorism and Political Turbulence;* CJCS Handbook 5260, *Commander's Handbook for Antiterrorism Readiness;* Joint Publication (JP) 3-0, *Doctrine for Joint Operations;* and JP 3-07, *Joint Doctrine for Military Operations Other than War.* The list also includes the basic doctrinal documents of each of the military services: AFDD 1, *Air Force Basic Doctrine;* Field Manual 100-5, *Operations;* NDP 1, *Naval Warfare;* and FMFM 1, *Warfighting.*

In order to fully satisfy the environmental criteria established in the last chapter, these documents must identify the environment in which AT must function, account for its ability to function in that environment at all times and allow for advances in technology. In keeping with the second part of the model, this doctrine must also fulfill the operational requirements by identifying linkages across the entire spectrum of military operations.

DoD Directive 2000.12 is the most senior relevant doctrine within the Department of Defense. In the physical environmental context, the directive allows for AT programs both overseas and in the continental United States, and extends applicability to all DoD personnel, families, and facilities regardless of military service.

To see how the doctrine covers the spectrum at the DoD level, DoD Directive 2000.12 specifies one indispensable piece of administrative minutiae necessary for every military operation; an organizational chart with associated responsibilities. A synthesis of this organization is shown in figure 3.

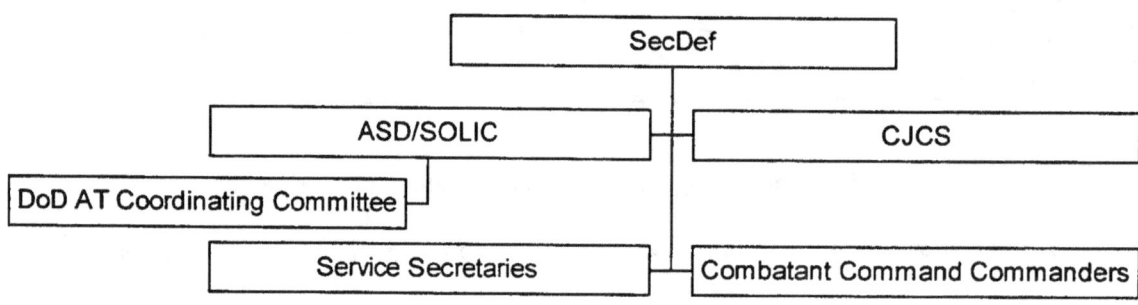

Figure 3 DoD AT Structure

Without going into excruciating detail, it assigns AT proponency and the lead role "to ensure compliance with this Directive by all DoD activities"[19] to the Assistant Secretary of Defense for Special Operations and Low-Intensity Conflict (ASD/SOLIC). The list of additional AT responsibilities for ASD/SOLIC is impressive, but can be summarized as fundamentally a staff function that is concerned with providing policy oversight and acting as the DoD focal point with external agencies. In fulfilling the criteria to be sensitive to technological changes, ASD/SOLIC also has a responsibility to coordinate with the Under Secretary of Defense

(Acquisition and Technology) on AT technology development and application of new technology to meet force protection needs.

DoD Directive 2000.12 also names the CJCS as the principal advisor to the Secretary of Defense for all AT issues. The CJCS develops the joint doctrine and AT standards, assesses AT measures for deploying and deployed forces, and evaluates the doctrine, standards, policies and programs of the services and the Combatant Commands. The CJCS is also charged with identifying AT requirements for the DoD budget process. This is a significant linkage between the tactical and the strategic levels of doctrine.

Through the service Secretaries, the individual services are tasked to develop and implement programs, train forces and commanders, and develop intelligence. In keeping with the general responsibilities of the services, they are tasked to identify resource requirements and program, plan and fund the various AT programs.

DoD Directive 2000.12 tasks the commanders-in-chief (CINCs) of the geographic combatant commands, the other half of the dual military structure, with identifying AT requirements to the services for action. The CINCs review and assesses the AT posture of all the military forces (excluding those specifically withheld by the Department of State (DoS)) within their respective area of operations (AOR). CINCs are also charged with reviewing the security measures for those DoS functions to make sure that adequate measures are in force. While the services or subordinate commands can make these assessments, a report must be made to the CINC regardless of the chain of command.

While on the topic of the chain of command, one of the most important AT functions the CINC provides is an assessment of the command relationships of organizations within the AOR so that a clear line of responsibility and accountability for protection is established.

One dichotomy in this arrangement is apparent; if the CINCs identify the requirement but the services must provide the solution through programming and budgeting, a delay will most likely occur as the matter is staffed through the various joint and service administrative functions. A one-stop-shopping approach would reduce the wait between identifying a requirement and implementing the solution.

As the senior Department of Defense guidance, this document would be the logical place to outline the interagency and multinational doctrinal basis. The document does prescribe DoD attendance at the Policy Coordinating Committee on Counterterrorism. The accompanying DoD 0-2000.12-H briefly outlines the composition and responsibilities of the major members of that group (see table 10) but does not detail the interactions between the agencies. Since this group makes policy recommendations, a firm understanding of the interrelations is critical, but lacking.

To observe any interagency guidance of substance at this level, one must refer to several memorandums of understanding between the State Department and the Department of Defense that are referenced in the DoD Directive 2000.12. One such agreement, the "Memorandum of Understanding Between the Department of State and the Department of Defense on Security on the Arabian Peninsula" was reached in the aftermath of the Khobar Towers tragedy. It is extremely limited in scope and only applies to that geographical area.

While a deeper discussion of the content and implications of this memorandum is reserved for later, let it suffice for now to acknowledge that with these exceptions, no other interagency agreements or doctrine is provided or referenced. What then guides the CINCs and their staffs in coordinating with the Central Intelligence Agency, the Department of Justice, or any of the other agencies listed? Similarly, the DoD Directive 2000.12 is devoid of any discussion of AT in multinational operations other than an admonishment to CINCs to "ensure that AT countermeasures are being coordinated with host-country agencies at all levels."[20] This represents a serious shortfall in the doctrine available to the military commander who relies on the combined abilities of the Department of Defense and the State Department to reach appropriate accords with multinational partners.

42

Table 10. PCC/CT Structure

Member	Key Responsibilities
Department of State	Chairs committee and subcommittee Conducts diplomatic AT efforts Leads development of AT assistance programs Lead agency for terrorist incidents overseas Identifies security needs for U.S. officials abroad Disseminates international threat information
Department of Justice FBI Drug Enforcement Agency Immigration and Naturalization Service U.S. Marshals Service	 Lead domestic law-enforcement agency Maintains civilian counterterrorist capabilities Assists the FAA with aviation security assessments Collects, analyzes and disseminates domestic threat information Provides terrorist information to other agencies Provides scientific and technical support Tracks international movement of specified individuals Tracks movement of specified individuals
Treasury Department U.S. Secret Service U.S. Customs Service Bureau of Alcohol, Tobacco, and Firearms	 Concerned with threats to protected key officials Collects, analyzes, and disseminates threat information Involved in security technology development Prevents movement of terrorist materiel into U.S. Controls export of potential terrorist materiel Participates in counterdrug operations Conducts AT research and development Provides terrorist information to other agencies. Provides technical and scientific support in the development of bomb detection systems. Investigates violations of federal weapons laws
Department of Transportation Federal Aviation Administration U.S. Coast Guard	 Domestic airport security Provides airport security expertise to other countries Lead agency for international incidents in flight Port and waterway security AT security standards for ships and navigational aids
Department of Energy	Collects, analyzes and disseminates information Wide range of specialized equipment and personnel Protects special materials against terrorists
CIA	Leads national-level collection, analysis, and dissemination
National Security Council	Coordination and policy studies

The most important contribution of the accompanying DoD 0-2000.12-H, other than being designated the DoD standard, is its comprehensive treatment of the entire spectrum of antiterrorism albeit subject to the same limitations previously discussed. By outlining the history and characteristics of terrorism, the U.S. policy, legal and regulatory guidelines, the threat analysis system, and a host of physical security measures this document actually spans the three levels of structure.

The CJCS Handbook 5260, *Commander's Handbook for Antiterrorism Readiness* represents the environmental doctrine promulgated by the CJCS and is addressed directly to the identified center of gravity, the commander. The DoD Directive 2000.12 initiated the writing of this document by designating the CJCS the DoD's principal for all AT force protection issues.

The CJCS certainly sets the correct tone by stating, "we must become preeminent in antiterrorism and force protection."[21] The publication addresses the environmental imperative under the declaration that force protection is, "the security program designed to protect soldiers, civilian employees, family members, facilities, and equipment in all locations and situations."[22] One certainly senses this is a nonstop activity that must occur on all fronts.

The CJCS Handbook 5260 is very thorough in its discussion of technology, especially with repeated references to the use of high technology by terrorists. Concern stems from the ease of obtaining state-of-the-art communications, surveillance and identification systems. The proposed response is to fight fire with fire, "As our technological capability increases, so does the need to apply these advances to combat terrorism."[23] To that end, the Joint Staff sponsors an annual Force Protection Technology Symposium where military and industry can meet and discuss requirements. Coupled with the Chairman's inherent authority to direct the Joint Requirements Oversight Council to include AT requirements in deliberating various acquisition programs, one can conclude this aspect of environmental doctrine provides a mechanism to put theory into practice.

The CJCS Handbook 5260 condenses and repeats the interagency information of the DoD 0-2000.12-H without adding anything more of substance. There is no requirement to establish any type of standardized interagency organization, either in the U.S. or overseas. In discussing the multinational aspect of AT, the document outlines the problem from a stationing requirement perspective but does nothing to address the issues, and completely ignores the multinational operations viewpoint.

Next is an analysis of JP 3-0. This document provides the "principles and doctrine for the conduct of joint and multinational operations." [24]Note the first mention of multinational operations. In defining the continuum of conflict, this document breaks down the range of military operations into two large categories, war and operations other than war. Recalling the requirement that antiterrorism activities must take place across the continuum, this doctrine should place AT in both categories. Unfortunately, it places antiterrorism in just the later category and as a discrete entity. (See figure 4.) While perhaps considered trite, the phrase, "a picture speaks a thousand words" applies to the context associated with this figure. If accepted blindly, this graphic reinforces a tendency to inappropriately compartmentalize AT efforts, disrupting the development of the proper mindset.

As currently written, the publication cautions joint force commanders to "take action to protect or shield all elements of the joint force from enemy symmetrical and asymmetrical action"[25] and they "must protect their forces and their freedom of action."[26] It tells commanders to protect their forces from the enemy's firepower and maneuver, see to the health, welfare, morale and maintenance of the applicable personnel, and dictates the integration of safety into all training and operations. It also contains a caveat that any noncombat operations can turn violent and all forces should take steps to protect themselves and respond to the changing environment. While all these items are certainly excellent components of force protection (and common sense), the antiterrorism component is conspicuous by its absence.

45

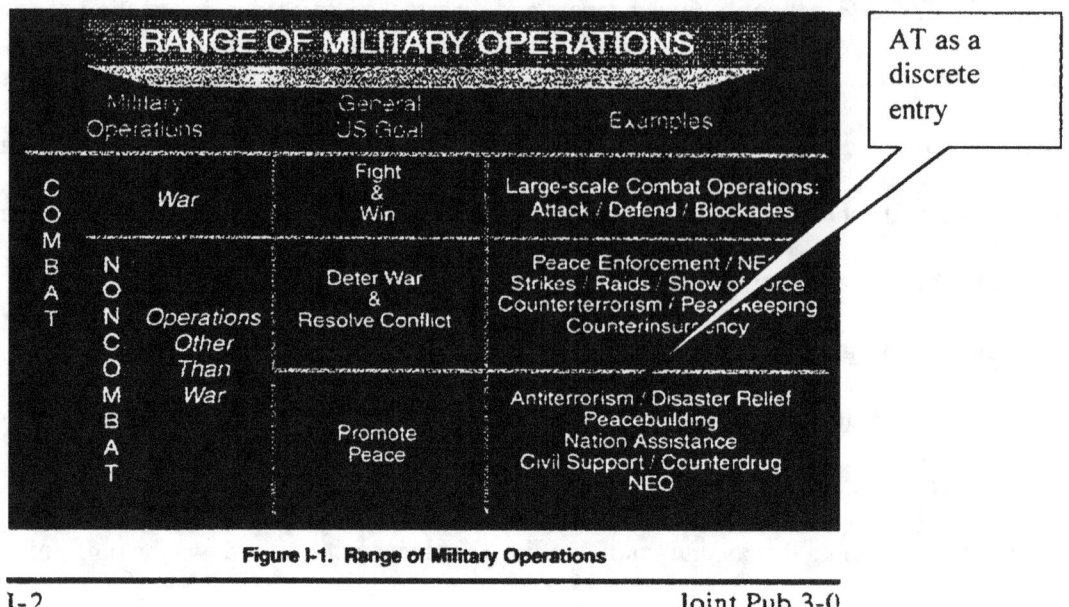

Figure 4. Extract from JP 3-0 page I-2.

Another interesting implication of JP 3-0 in its treatment of combatting terrorism is identifying it as a particular operation rather than an integral part of all operations. While particular aspects of combatting terrorism can be considered in a single-operation framework, the requirements for valid environmental doctrine demand its application across the continuum.

JP 3-0 devotes an entire chapter to multinational operations, the most comprehensive treatment thus far. While explicit discussions of AT in this environment are absent, the publication lays the groundwork by outlining this environment in detail. Additionally, it tasks commanders to work with the local security forces for protection and indicates joint protection requirements and practices are directly transferable to the multinational arena. Understanding the publication was referring to protection in combat, one could take exception to this extension of logic in the AT battle. While the purpose of AT remains the same, implementing prudent AT programs would definitely be complicated in a multinational environment like the one described in the opening vignette of this study. However, this chapter can be used as a model for developing more robust AT doctrine in a multinational setting.

JP 3-07, *Joint Doctrine for Military Operations other than War* (commonly referred to as MOOTW) is the document that assigns AT to a MOOTW environment under the umbrella term "combatting terrorism." Its one paragraph contribution discusses how AT programs form the basis for all efforts to combat terrorism and necessitates the balancing between the ways, means, and ends of preventing terrorism. Interestingly enough, the reproduction of the "range of military operations" graphic from JP 3-0 and used in the previous section appears in this publication with the antiterrorism reference completely absent. During the discussion of the security for employed forces, military members are reminded to be prepared for the potential of any situation to turn violent and reiterates the inherent right to self defense.

There are some extremely limited references to planning and conducting generic interagency and multinational operations, but the utility is limited to acknowledging other agencies could be involved and in command. The only practical consideration was identifying the increased requirement for liaisons.

Clearly, this publication fails to explicitly meet all criteria except the implied joint applicability of AT. Perhaps the relevant service doctrine can provide the necessary requirements. For convenience, one can safely assume the service doctrine by definition meets the unilateral employment criteria.

Air Force doctrine is generally less developed than the corresponding writings in the Army. It has undergone substantial revisions in recent years. The fundamental doctrine manual, AFDD 1 acquits itself well when discussing combatting terrorism in macro terms. While following the trend of the higher-order and other services doctrine, the Air Force places combatting terrorism under the auspices of MOOTW. By using a "caution" (a term instantly recognized in the Air Force culture to denote a practice or procedure significant enough to emphasize) the manual instantly brings the serious nature of the threat. Specifically, "Caution: A distinct characteristic of MOOTW is the ever-existing possibility that any type of MOOTW may quickly change from noncombat to combat and vice versa. Regardless, use of appropriate self-defense measures are always authorized."[27] Further, the writing expresses quite clearly, "airmen must understand that violence (and casualties) may occur in virtually any type of operation and, therefore, must be ready and able at all times to defend themselves and their units."[28] Unfortunately, the assignment of AT to the specific category of MOOTW clashes with this latter philosophy.

On the technology aspect, the newness of the Air Force doctrine derives a benefit from familiarity with *Joint Vision 2010*, the CJCS' joint military vision of the future. In *Joint Vision 2010*, all the operational concepts that will shape future operations are wrapped in a band of technological innovation. As this concept is embedded in the Air Force doctrine, it would implicitly apply to AT activities. Most assuredly, the other services will follow suit as their doctrine is updated to conform to the joint master plan.

AFDD 1 acknowledges the Air Force will most likely be employed in a joint environment, but is mute on interagency and multinational considerations.

The U.S. Army has by far the most voluminous basic doctrine of any service, and therefore one would hope it was similarly the most inclusive of antiterrorism material. A review of FM 100-5 finds an excellent understanding of antiterrorism:

> During peacetime, the Army combats terrorism primarily through antiterrorism, which are those passive defensive measures taken to minimize vulnerability to terrorism. Antiterrorism is a form of force protection and, thus, the responsibility of Army commanders at all levels. Antiterrorism complements counterterrorism, which is the full range of offensive measures taken to prevent, deter, and respond to terrorism. Army elements, such as SOF, assist in this interagency effort by applying specialized capabilities to preclude, preempt, and resolve terrorist incidents abroad. Counterterrorism occurs in conflict and war; antiterrorism occurs across the range of military operations.

Certainly this doctrine reflects a close fit to the environmental requirements of applicability at all locations at all times with a clear chain of responsibility through commanders at all levels. However, as with the Air Force example, contradictions can be perceived. Although explicitly stated as AT "occurs across the range of military operations" the doctrine insists on relegating the discussion to the chapter on operations other than war, treating it like a separate operation, and graphically depicting it one dimensionally, much like the figure in JP 3-0.

The Army doctrine presents the best case by far for implicitly and explicitly setting the conditions for the use of technology in the AT environment. In general it says "Doctrine should reflect new technology and its potential for the future."[29] This statement frames the outlook that both doctrine writers and innovators of technology should have. Specifically, "It sets the conditions to exploit technologies that . . . offers major improvements for protection to forces."[30] Clearly this criterion has been met.

The Army also has the most comprehensive guidance of any service on joint and combined (multinational operations) by devoting two chapters to the subjects, although without reference to AT. Even so, that treatment would make an excellent base for overlaying the AT requirements. In what seems to be a trend, interagency doctrine that could support AT efforts is lacking.

The United States Navy is in the process of developing coherent doctrine in a series of six capstone documents. While the most useful (and consistent) evaluation for this study would be an analysis of NDP 3, *Naval Operations*, that document has not yet been published. Therefore, the study will refer to NDP 1 *Naval Warfare* in an attempt to meet the specifications. In viewing this as environmental doctrine, it very specifically aligns naval operations to the sea and the surrounding environs. It is a self-described operational document, used to bridge the gap between the strategic and the tactical levels of operations.

In the AT context, the publication does reference the acknowledged international right of a nation to combat terrorism. Consistent with the other services' doctrine, the Navy places this function under the category of "Naval Operations--Other Than War." Other references addresses the use of naval forces in a deterrence role (i.e., retaliation for terrorist attacks) and to employ

49

forces in a counterterrorism role[31] but virtually ignores any doctrinal reference to force protection in general or antiterrorism specifically. In a rather surprising observation, there are extremely limited discussions of the role of any technology in this warfighting philosophy of the Navy. In fact, the term itself only appears twice in the entire document, and neither in an AT context.

In the now well developed pattern, the doctrine does address the requirement for American forces to work in a joint or combined environment, but once again missed any reference to interagency activities. All told, it is obvious to see that NDP 1 has no emphasis and little applicability in the quest for adequate organizational AT doctrine.

U.S. Marine Corp doctrine is the last to be examined with FMFM 1, *Warfighting*. First, in a discussion of the fundamental nature of the environment in which Marines may be called upon to fight, there is an acknowledgement that, "war may range from intense clashes between large military forces backed by an official declaration of war to covert hostilities which barely reach the threshold of violence."[32] A discussion on the nature of war indicates it can be waged by any group, state-sponsored or independent of a nation-state, that is capable of generating violence to further their goals. Here is implicit guidance that terrorism lies within the spectrum of Marine operations and should be addressed accordingly. Another good (although implicit) discussion of terrorism is represented in the following: "Many political groups simply do not possess the military means to wage war at the high end of the spectrum. Many who fight a technologically or numerically superior enemy may choose to fight in a way that does not justify the enemy's full use of that superiority."[33]

The Marines have an excellent representation of the role of technology in their efforts. In the chapter on equipping the Marine force, the doctrine warns simultaneously against overreliance and failing to take full advantage of technology. The dangers of overreliance are simple; a countermeasure will be discovered and implemented by the enemy or the technology will fail when one needs it most. Failure to exploit the best this country has to offer can needlessly place American troops in harms way.

Interestingly enough, the Marine Corp doctrine spends very little time and effort discussing anything other than unilateral actions. The document references joint issues only twice; once in a statement that Marine doctrine is in concert with joint doctrine and once to enjoin senior Marine commanders to be experts in integrating Marine capabilities into joint and multinational operations. That is also the only reference to any multinational requirements. It is completely mute on interagency capabilities or synergies. One cannot help leave the Marine Corps' premier doctrine on warfighting without the image of the king's champion engaging in single combat.

This concludes the evaluation of the environmental doctrine. Highlighting the important findings, there is a consistent gap in the doctrine to apply antiterrorism efforts across the entire operational spectrum at all times. Similarly, there is very little guidance in the form of interagency or multinational operations. These are obvious places for doctrinal improvement. The findings are summarized in table 11.

Table 11. Environmental/Operational Score Card

	DoD 2000.12 and DoD 0-2000.12-H	CJCS HANDBOOK 5260	JP 3-0	JP 3-07	AFDD 1	FM 100-5	NDP 1	FMFM 1
Environmental Structure Criteria								
Worldwide applicability in all mediums at all times	+	+	-	-	+	+	-	-
Covers entire spectrum of operations and all levels of violence	+	+	-	-	+	+	-	-
Incorporates emerging technologies	+	+	-	-	+	+	-	+
Operational Content Criteria								
Unilateral employment	+	-	-	-	+	+	+	+
Joint employment	+	+	+	+	+	+	+	-
Interagency agreements	+	+	-	-	-	-	-	-
Multinational considerations	-	-	+	-	-	+	+	-

The Leaves: Organizational and Tactical Doctrine

The last category of doctrine that requires evaluation is that of the organizational type. Again, this should be a narrowly focused effort, depicting what a particular organization (including joint commands) will do at a particular time. This can be identified as the tactics, techniques, and procedures (TTP) associated with the joint and service policies and programs. The relevant publications for evaluation are Joint Publication 3-07.2, *JTTP for Antiterrorism*, and the service's subordinate AT-specific doctrine. Each will be discussed briefly in turn. Additional doctrine, such as physical protection measures, engineering support, etc., while important, are beyond the scope of this study.

JP 3-07.2 was to represents the capstone tactical AT doctrine at the joint level. However, contrary to expectations, this document exhibits the attributes of all three categories and functions simultaneously, much like the DoD 0-2000.12-H. The beginning paragraphs shows its purpose is to "provides commanders guidance on how to organize, plan and train for the employment of U.S. forces in interagency and multinational antiterrorism operations."[34] The document than goes into significant detail on the national strategy, DoD, CJCS, ASD/SOLIC, and the CINCs' role in AT, spends considerable effort discussing the legal restrictions and outlines a hierarchy of detailed AT programs.

By far, this is the most comprehensive AT document analyzed. Even so, this voluminous publication cautions that it is not a stand-alone document; it must be consolidated with other service and agency publications in order to provide comprehensive coverage.

With all its credits, there are some obvious shortfalls in this document. First, it has not been updated since written in June of 1993. Therefore, it misses the 1996 revisions in the DoD Directive 2000.12. The most significant discrepancy is that the DoD Directive 2000.12 designates its accompanying handbook as "the standard that shall apply to all AT force protection efforts of the Department of Defense."[35] This conflicts with the avowed statement of purpose in

JP 3-07.2. The implication is that there are two manuals claiming primacy, with the one most accessible to commanders (the joint publication) wrongly claiming that responsibility.

This document, implicitly under the joint publication numbering system and explicitly in the text, assigns antiterrorism to the auspices of joint operations in low intensity conflict. The same arguments as to the need to specify AT activities across the spectrum can be made to reinforce the problems inherent in this association. First, the force protection aspects of antiterrorism programs exist simultaneously in the unilateral (service) and joint arenas.

Second, the document reiterates the proponency of ASD/SOLIC for antiterrorism policy. Both of these associations tend to create a mindset in which antiterrorism can be viewed as in the "special operations" domain and not the mainstream where it belongs. The flaw is self-evident when the document contradicts itself by making the assertion that terrorism is a factor across the entire operational continuum.

The organizational layer of Air Force antiterrorism doctrine is Air Force Instruction 31-210, *The Air Force Antiterrorism Program*. This doctrine outlines the responsibilities of major commands and field operating agencies to "establish an antiterrorism program tailored to the local mission, conditions, and the terrorist threat."[36] It assigns various responsibilities to staff functions and relevant headquarters. The instruction establishes the Headquarters Air Force Director of Security Forces as the focal point for all Air Force AT matters. It also charges installation commanders to implement a local program applicable to their local threat in concert with the Air Force program. While the individual Air Force member's responsibilities are not listed per se, the importance of individual training and awareness is actualized through specific training requirements.

In the tactical sense, the Air Force does an outstanding job of relying on the mandated DoD standards of establishing threat conditions (THREATCONS) and Random Antiterrorism Measures (RAM) in accordance with the DoD 0-2000.12-H.

The Army AT perspective is contained within AR 525-13. The doctrine assigns an Army proponent (the Deputy Chief of Staff for Operations and Plans--a level significantly higher than the Air Force proponent), assigns responsibilities to specific headquarters, staff organizations, and commanders. The doctrine makes a clean distinction between actions and responsibilities of deployed and nondeployed commanders, setting specific circumstances and specifying echelons from corps through battalions. This is the most comprehensive of all organizational doctrine. The treatment of individual soldier responsibilities is parallel with the Air Force; recognition that training is required for all personnel.

While the Army doctrine closely follows the DoD 0-2000.12-H in many respects, it too predates the designation of the DoD standards and therefore does not explicitly accede to the Secretary of Defense's mandate.

As previously mentioned, there is no U.S. Navy equivalent document. This does not imply the Navy ignores AT activities like physical security and law enforcement requirements. Quite the contrary; the Navy has very comprehensive guidance in that regard. It simply means there is no Navy-wide comprehensive AT guidance for use at the tactical level. Subordinate levels, such as numbered fleets, may publish such information.

The Marine Corp has its FMFRP 7-14A, *The Individual's Guide for Understanding and Surviving Terrorism.* This doctrine, while full of practical guidelines to preclude or mitigate terrorist activity against an individual, does little to fulfill the organizational requirements. First, as the title implies, the doctrine is geared for the individual Marine. There is no assigned proponent. It does not assign responsibilities to unit or installation commanders. While personal awareness is a keystone of AT programs, it is impossible to assign primary AT responsibility to every individual. Command programs and policies must be implemented for a comprehensive AT environment to be built. While the document implies terrorist activity could occur at any time, it does not reference or make use of the THREATCON or RAM processes common in the

DoD, Air Force, and Army doctrine. It does not mandate compliance with the DoD standards. The Marines are in the process of developing a Marine Corp reference publication on combatting terrorism that should be on a par with the Air Force and Army documents and should prescribe compliance with the appropriate standards.

In summary, the most telling result of this analysis was to discover that JP 3-07.2 actually transcends the structure and content model postulated. As such, it should be updated and coupled with the DoD 0-2000.12-H to eliminate any redundancy and streamline the process. The other finding shows a need to update all the service publications (except the Air Force). The results are captured in table 12.

Table 12. Organizational/Tactical Score Card

	JP 3-07.2	AFI 31-210	AR 525-13	U.S.N.	FMFRP 7-14A
Organizational Structure Criteria					
Acknowledged existence	+	+	+	-	+
Tactical Content Criteria					
TTPs meet DoD standards	-	+	-	-	-

The Roots: Intelligence versus the Threat

A brief history of the terrorism that builds to the present-day threat to national security is in order to understand how the AT doctrinal tree is rooted in intelligence. Terrorism can trace its roots to ancient times with attendant evolutionary changes in motives and methods occurring with the passage of time. Aristotle wrote in *Politics Book V* about terror tactics used by tyrannical rulers of the day to establish and maintain their power. The *Sicarri* were a religious sect employing terrorist tactics to advance their views during the Zealot struggle in Palestine in AD 66-73.[37] The *Assassins* dominated terror in Persia and Syria from the eleventh through the thirteenth centuries, murdering their enemies as a religious duty or for hire, coining the term still in use today.[38] In 1881 Alexander II, Tsar of Russia, was assassinated by a terrorist determined to overthrow the tsarist system of government.[39] In 1914, a Serbian nationalist killed the heir apparent to the Austro-Hungarian Empire, which in turn used the incident as an excuse to begin World War I.[40] One cannot help but conclude that terrorists always have and always will be part of the human condition and can profoundly impact societies.

In a more contemporary light, terrorism burst onto the international scene via satellite television in the September 1972 attack on the Olympic Games in Munich. The Black September Organization, an anti-Israeli group, claimed responsibility.[41] This attack was to set the stage for the next twenty years. This style was typified by activities carried out internationally and characterized by attempts to dominate the media and sway public opinion in the favor of the terrorists' cause. Terrorists (with noted exceptions) were not generally suicidal but created elaborate plans to escape after their activities.

The collapse of the Soviet Union (recognized as a significant sponsor of international terrorism) and international cooperation geared to condemning terrorism and denying terrorists safe havens have fundamentally altered the terrorism environment. Ideologically motivated terrorism has been in a decline while religious fervor is reemerging and setting new standards in terrorist activities. Noted terrorism expert Stefan Leaders said: "Evidence increasingly suggests that religiously motivated terrorists are much less interested in drawing attention to themselves and their cause and more interested in punishing adversaries by killing large numbers of people."[42]

Coupled with Mr. Leader's assessment is concern that technology is allowing this ancient motivation to manifest itself in a more destructive fashion. Ambassador Phillip Wilcox, the Presidential and State Department's Coordinator for Counterterrorism outlines the heightened threat of weapons of mass destruction.

Now, conventional explosives are readily available and the technology to make them and, worse yet, terrorists have increasing access to materials of mass destruction--nuclear, chemical and biological. In today's volatile mix of religious fanaticism, pathological terrorists and other dangerous and perverse forces and their access to modern technology increases the danger of terrorism tremendously. Terrorists not only have access to these materials of technological resources, another form of technology--the expansion of international media and communications--gives them a much, much broader stage upon which to perform, to intimidate, and to terrorize.[43]

Other highly placed officials and experts agree that the threat by weapons of mass destruction (WMD) is growing. In a sense, a tripwire was broken on 20 March 1995 when sarin nerve gas was released in the Tokyo subway system, killing nine and injuring over 5,500 people. The apocalyptic religious sect Aum Shinrikyo (translated as "Supreme Truth") was indicted in the attack. Police raids on Aum property yielded tons of chemicals that could be used to produce more of the deadly poison.[44] Chemical weapons have been used in a terrorist attack; are biological or even nuclear weapons next?

The world is witnessing an evolution in terrorism characterized by larger scale, more indiscriminate (and more publicized) violence as a result of exploitation of technology. The United States must prevent the use of weapons of mass destruction against American interests. Most significantly, the motivation of the terrorist has changed. Ideology and nationalism are being replaced by extremism. The State Department captured the essence of the climate in stating, "The death toll form acts of international terrorism rose from 163 in 1995 to 311 in 1996, as the trend continued toward more ruthless attacks on mass civilian targets and the use of more powerful bombs. The threat of terrorist use of materials of mass destruction is an issue of growing concern."[45]

This threat reiterates the need for an intelligence structure at all levels of operations. The requirements for this type of intelligence can be assigned to the structure of the fundamental, environmental, and organizational framework without the exhaustive analysis. The fundamental doctrine (specifically PDD 39) tasks the Director of Central Intelligence with "leading the efforts of the Intelligence Community to reduce U.S. vulnerabilities to international terrorism."[46] With the understanding that the Defense Intelligence Agency (DIA) is the major DoD component of the national intelligence community, the President's declaration provides the structure for DoD to share in the national intelligence capabilities. This is certainly consistent with a recommendation by the Long Commission discussed in the next chapter.

At the environmental level, DoD Directive 2000.12 prescribes a robust internal role for the DIA in coordinating AT intelligence requirements. The DIA "is the focal point within the Department of Defense for data and information pertaining to domestic and foreign terrorist threats to DoD personnel."[47] Also at this level and the organizational level, each service is tasked with building a capability to "collect, receive, and evaluate, from a service perspective, and disseminate all relevant data on terrorist activities, trends, and indicators of imminent attack."[48] Furthermore, theater CINCs are required to assess the threat within the theater, issue the appropriate assessment to the services, subordinate commanders, and the chiefs of mission within the AOR. They make sure the local commanders are prepared and capable of responding to a changing threat environment. The DoD 0-2000.12-H also tasks the DIA with representing DoD in the National Intelligence Terrorism Warning process, an interagency intelligence fusion system.

The Soil: Capabilities and Restrictions

Unfortunately, the U.S. military does not have carte blanche in which to build the ultimate antiterrorist capability. While exploring the authority vested in a commander, this section will also address the doctrinal restrictions, constraints, and limits placed on the commander and how are they overcome.

Within the United States. Section 797 of Title 50 of the United States Code, known as *The Internal Security Act of 1950*, has granted extraordinary authority to military installation commanders within the United States to maintain law and order and protect the people and the resources on their installations. This authority extends to the use of deadly force under certain circumstances foreseeable in the AT environment. However, this authority ends at the perimeter of the installation. Even with that statutory authority, commanders still must rigidly observe the Constitution and the applicable laws and regulations.

While responsible for installation security itself, the installation commander by law must rely on civilian law enforcement agencies for the AT protection measures off the installation. Within the United States, the Department of Justice (and specifically the FBI) is the lead federal agency for terrorism within the United States. The FBI is specifically charged with acquiring terrorist information and intelligence in the U.S. This arrangement can place several burdens on the commander. Obviously, the commander does not have any authority over the civilian agencies. Second, military personnel must remain under military command and control. Equivalently, civilian personnel cannot be used by the military commander without special arrangements being approved. Third, the military is extremely limited in their ability to conduct intelligence-gathering operations in this country. Military commanders and members must scrupulously observe the limitations imposed by various laws and regulations, including: Executive Order 12333, *United States Intelligence Activities;* DoD Directive 5240.1, *DoD Intelligence Activities;* DoD Regulation 52401-R, *Activities of DoD Intelligence Components That Affect United States Persons*, and all applicable service regulations.

State and local authorities also play a significant role, albeit a very diverse one that is dependent on the specific situation. Its interesting to note DoD 0-2000.12-H says, "The role of state and local law enforcement agencies is more difficult. Within this gray area, no clear rules or guidelines exists."[49]

How are these issues resolved? Army AT doctrine addresses these problems best. Army installation commanders are specifically expected to coordinate their local AT plans with the FBI, state and local officials. These agencies are provided copies of those plans when security considerations permit. Left unsaid in the Army doctrine is the requirement for commanders to establish good dialogue and rapport with these agencies and have standing mechanisms for an effective interface to exchange information and address concerns.

What about the situations in which commanders have personnel that routinely work externally to a military installation? Examples would include recruiters working in a leased commercial office or instructors assigned to the local college's Reserve Officer Training Corps. Again, the commanders must work with the appropriate civilian agencies and possibly even the landlord in an ad hoc effort to gain the best possible security.

Outside of the United States. For forces stationed or deployed outside of CONUS, the "primary responsibility for responding to overseas terrorist treats or attacks rests with the host country."[50] Usually, the associated issues are outlined in international agreements such as Status of Forces Agreements, bilateral, and multinational stationing agreements. The commander must always remember that the host country has both the right and the legitimate authority to enforce their laws and enforce security procedures, even on the U.S. installation in the host country. This right of sovereign power may impact on the ability of the U.S. authorities to prevent terrorist attacks. This could contradict or invalidate procedures that are used routinely inside the United States. For example, a particular antiterrorism measure (external surveillance of the base's perimeter) may be invalid (and illegal) under the governing international agreement that permits U.S. forces to occupy the base.

It is incumbent upon all commanders to have an absolute understanding of the legal issues involved and their authority in this situation. Relying on the efficiency and good will of the host country to provide security "outside the fence" is apt to make any commander uncomfortable, even when dealing with staunch allies like the United Kingdom or Germany. It is doubly troubling when the host country is not well developed or is distracted by internal troubles (as in the Beirut case study). Again, as in the domestic arena, the commander cannot rely on authority but must depend on influence. It is critical that commanders appreciate that a positive, well-grounded working relationship with their host nation counterparts can influence the positioning of American forces, the resources the host nation expends on AT measures, and priorities and enhancements as the threat grows. The gentle art of negotiation can play a key role in these issues, especially the selection of the location of American operations.

Another issue associated with forces outside of the United States is the role of the DoS. DoS operations impact the U.S. military AT effort in three categories. First, DoS is designated by *PDD 39* as the lead federal agency for terrorism outside of the United States. While it may appear to military commanders that balancing the need for security with the need for diplomacy and protocol might be inherently difficult, they can take solace that the guidance from the President sets the correct priority. *PDD 39* states on the first page, "We shall work closely with friendly governments in carrying out our counterterrorism policy."

Second, DoS negotiates those international agreements governing U.S. forces in host countries. It is imperative that commanders provide the unique military perspective and requirements to the State Department both during negotiations and later as shortfalls and problems appear. For those seemingly insurmountable problems, commander always retain the right to elevate issues through their chain of command to the theater CINC for resolution. Almost always in practice however, commanders will find themselves working for the same end-state as their State Department counterpart and significant disputes should be few and far between.

Third, "pursuant to 22 U.S.C. Section 4802, the Secretary of State is responsible . . . for developing and implementing policies and programs to provide for the security of DoD elements and personnel not under the command of the CINC." To understand the context of this statement, it must be understood that military personnel assigned overseas fall under either the DoD structure through the statutory combatant command authority of the theater CINC or are directly assigned to a particular ambassador and the applicable country team. In the former, AT protection is the responsibility of the CINC; the State Department is responsible in the latter case. To further cloud the issue, each service has worldwide AT responsibilities for their respective installations.

This division of responsibility could easily cause a gap in AT protection measures. This "invitation to struggle" has not gone unnoticed. Following the Khobar Towers attack, the respective Secretaries formalized a "Memorandum of Understanding Between the Department of State and the Department of Defense on Security on the Arabian Peninsula" that would preclude any particular unit or person from falling through any gaps in the security net. Unfortunately, this memorandum is limited geographically to the seven countries of the Arabian Peninsula.

The last issue associated with forces and installations external to CONUS is the responsibility for intelligence gathering. The Central Intelligence Agency plays an analogous role to the FBI when conducting overseas intelligence operations. Again, numerous laws and regulations dictate DoD involvement; the same ones that were specified in the domestic context plus Public Law 95-511, *The Foreign Intelligence Surveillance Act of 1978*. Commanders are responsible to comply with the "substantive and procedural requirements of these references while conducting intelligence activities."[51]

Regardless of the laws, regulations, and relations between nations, the bottom line is that the U.S. commander "retains the responsibility for the safety and security of personnel and property on U.S. installations outside U.S. territory."[52] Endowed with this responsibility without necessarily having the requisite authority is a serious injustice to American commanders.

Commanders are faced with another significant restraint on their ability to implement antiterrorism programs and policies. Increased AT efforts are usually accompanied by a corresponding decrease in the efficiency of operations. This is an expected cause-effect relationship; AT efforts are designed to make it more difficult for a terrorist to conduct operations so an attended level of inconvenience to all affected personnel (and families, installation visitors, contractors, etc.) is a logical result. In the most extreme circumstances, a commander could essentially close down an installation, bringing all activity to a halt while instigating the most rigorous AT procedures. Additionally, one reaches a point of diminishing returns with regard to increasing security where the additional expenditure of time, personnel, or money will only bring about microscopic increases in protection. When is that point reached? All these issues are the responsibility of the commander who must "balance increased security measures with the loss of effectiveness during prolonged operations and the accompanying impact on quality-of-life."[53]

AT is by no means commanders' only concern. Environmental, quality of life, personnel, and mission-related problems are just some of the other issues competing for commanders' time, attention, and resources. The truly skilled commander is the one adept at balanced all the competing demands and assigning the appropriate priority.

In summary, commanders appear to be hamstrung by restrictions when considering AT issues. In reality, it is no worse than implementing any other type of program; commanders must balance a multitude of issues. The major difference is the consequences of failure.

The Sap: Security

The study established in the previous chapter that articulating certain "principles of war" is a long-standing tradition in military doctrine writing. As such, the principle of *security* as embodied in force protection activities was shown to have particular relevance to the AT environment.

The DoD Directive 2000.12 and the DoD 0-2000.12-H contain numerous linkages between AT and force protection but fail to further link them to the fundamental principle of war. Again, this in indicative of a mindset in which AT is compartmentalized as a separate and distinct program not necessarily integrated into every operation.

The force protection theme is carried through the discussion of the Air Force's definition of the security principle of war in AFDD 1. It establishes Air Force people, equipment, and operations must be protected to prevent the enemy from acquiring an unexpected advantage. The doctrine points out this enemy could be military, paramilitary, groups or individuals and thus reinforces the idea that U.S. forces are vulnerable across the spectrum of military activity and location. This is the best representation of the correct relationship within the body of the doctrine. If only this sentiment was not at odds with the established categorization of AT under MOOTW.

A discussion of the principles of war indicates they are the bedrock of Army doctrine. In Army parlance, security "enhances freedom of action by reducing vulnerability to hostile acts, influence, or surprise. Security results from the measures taken by a commander to protect his forces."[54] Implicitly, this statement sets the conditions for the introduction of force protection and AT, however those concepts are not developed in that context. Force protection is alluded to in discussions of battlefield survivability and mentioned briefly in the AT paragraph, but is developed most extensively under the discussion of generic protection under combat conditions. That discussion lists four main areas of force protection: operations security, health and morale, safety, and avoidance of fratricide. This indicates the Army has an excellent understanding of the need for force protection, it is just lacking in the consistent doctrinal comprehension that force protection and AT must exist at all times and in all circumstances.

A discussion of the security principle of war does enjoin naval commanders in that protecting the force increases combat power but does so in the context of fleet actions and conventional military forces, not in protecting against terrorist attacks.

Although lower-level doctrine was purposely excluded from this study, it is instructive at this point to view the discussion of force protection in Navy Doctrine Publication 2:

> Force Protection. Force protection is both offensive and defensive. . . . These protect information against espionage, personnel against subversion and terrorism, and installations and material against sabotage. Adversary forces can be expected to use every available means to thwart or otherwise impede the operations of our naval forces. . . . Force protection encompasses the measures taken by the commander to protect his

forces, posture and information, and to deny such protection to his adversary. The commander must consider force protection in every aspect of planning and tailor it to the intended operations and the adversary's capabilities.[55]

This excellent passage illustrates that the correct identification and redress for the problem is in fact in the doctrine, but that it is not consistent and is not in the place it belongs!

The basic doctrine of the Marine Corp doesn't even address the security principle of war in any context, as does all the basic doctrine of the other services. This is a remarkable observation, especially in light of the Beirut attack. This represents a critical shortfall in setting the correct mindset for the relevant commanders.

A Summary of the Evaluation of the Doctrine

It is now possible to answer the leading questions of this chapter. First, the study sought to discover if the doctrine could be described in the context of a fundamental, environmental and organizational model. It was a successful effort in demonstrating that such a construction was a valid way to organize the writings. The notable exceptions were the DoD 0-2000.12-H and JP 3-07.2. Each of these documents showed a considerable range of content that could accurately be said to span the three levels. This characteristic has certain benefits to the commander, not least of which are fostering a greater understanding at the joint level and easing the administrative burden when studying the doctrine for applicability.

In applying the set strategic, operational and tactical requirements to the doctrine, there are shortfalls in each category. At the strategic level, the most significant discrepancy was a lack of clear articulation of the priority of AT efforts compared to other competing security requirements and the accompanying lack of prioritization of national resources. In the expressed formula, the end-state was correctly articulated, but the ways and means were not fully developed.

Overall, the DoD Directive 2000.12, associated DoD 0-2000.12-H, and the CJCS Handbook 5260 do an adequate job of filling the environmental and operational imperatives. It is when JP 3-0 and JP 3-07 are examined that the thread of continuity is lost. The most important flaw with this environmental doctrine is the lack of consistent understanding and articulation that AT efforts must span the continuum of conflict and operations. It should not be relegated to military operations other than war, it should not be thought of as a discrete operation in just a specific category, and it must not be exclusively associated with the special operations mindset. The Air Force and Army service doctrines both come the closest to the correct articulation, but both insist on retaining AT explicitly under the specific MOOTW category, other statements to the contrary notwithstanding. The Navy and Marine Corps doctrine is essentially immature and therefore of negligible value.

Finally at the operational level, there was a consistent lack of doctrine addressing interagency and multinational considerations. Even when these topics were addressed, it was a cursory treatment, devoid of any useful guidance.

The tactical analysis shows a consistent need for the services to comply with the promulgated DoD standards. This does not preclude the services to augment and improve the tactics, techniques, and procedures but adherence to the standard does provide a common understanding for the joint force commander.

In summarizing the roots, soil, and sap, considerable doctrinal issues need to be addressed. The threat has been shown to be growing and evolving and the doctrine appears to recognize that, at least at the higher levels. Commanders have a variety of intelligence and other resources to apply to the problem; prioritization is the key. The most significant weak link is the general lack of authority of the commander outside the military installation. Finally, the concept of security is not firmly imbedded in the doctrine and therefore not in the forefront of the commander's mindset where it belongs.

---

[1]Michael Howard, "Military Science in an Age of Peace," *Journal of the Royal United*

Services Institute for Defense Studies, in *Book of Readings: The Evolution of Modern Warfare (Term I)*, (Fort Leavenworth, Kansas: U.S. Army Command and General Staff College, 1997), 28.

[2]William J. Clinton, Presidential Decision Directive 39,: *U.S. Policy on Counterterrorism*, (Washington, DC: The White House, 21 June 1995), 1.

[3]George Bush, *Public Report of the Vice President's Task Force on Combatting Terrorism*, (Washington, DC: The White House, February 1986), 7.

[4]Bush, 9.

[5]General John M. Shalikashvili, *National Military Strategy*, (Washington, DC: Office of the Chairman of the Joint Chiefs of Staff, 1997), 14.

[6]Shalikashvili, 12.

[7]Bush, 21.

[8]William J. Clinton, *National Security Strategy for a New Century*, (Washington, DC: The White House, May 1997), 3.

[9]Shalikashvili, 10.

[10]Clinton, *U.S. Policy on Counterterrorism*, 2.

[11]Ibid., 3.

[12]Clinton, *National Security Strategy*, 9.

[13]Bush, 7.

[14]Shalikashvili, 6.

[15]Clinton, *U.S. Policy on Counterterrorism*, 10.

[16]Clinton, *National Security Strategy*, 9.

[17]Judy L. Thomas, "Hunt for terrorists has surged since blast Oklahoma City explosion spurred pre-emptive strategy by FBI, others," *Kansas City Star*, 19 April 1998, A-9.

[18]"The Real Battle," *U.S. News and World Report*, 27 April 1998, 7.

[19]Secretary of Defense, DoD Directive 2000.12, *DoD Combating Terrorism Program*, (Washington, DC: DoD, 15 September 1996), 3.

[20]DoD Directive 2000.12, 19.

[21]CJCSH 5260, i.

[22]Ibid., 20.

[23]Ibid., 21.

[24]JP 3-0, i.

[25]JP 3-0, p III-15.

[26]JP 3-0, p IV-3.

[27]U.S. Air Force, AFDD 1, *Basic Doctrine* (Washington, DC: Department of the Air Force, September 1997), 8.

[28]Ibid., 9.

[29]FM 100-5, 1-2.

[30]Ibid.

[31]U.S. Navy, NDP 1, *Naval Warfare* (Washington, DC: Department of the Navy, 18 March 1984), 19.

[32]U.S. Marine Corps, MCDP 1, *Warfighting* (Washington, DC: Department of the Navy, 20 June 1997), 4.

[33]Ibid., 12.

[34]Joint Staff, Joint Publication 3-07.2, *Joint Tactics, Techniques and Procedures for Antiterrorism* (Washington, DC: DoD, 25 June 1993), i.

[35]DoD Directive 2000.12, 2.

[36]U.S. Air Force, Air Force Instruction 31-210, *The Air Force Antiterrorism (AT) Program* (Washington, DC: Department of the Air Force, 1 July 1997), 2.

[37]Walter Laqueur and Yonah Alexander, *The Terrorism Reader* (New York: Penguin Books, 1987), 7.

[38]*New Encyclopedia Britannica*, 15th ed., "Terrorism."

[39]Franklin L. Ford, *Political Murder: From Tyrannicide to Terrorism* (Cambridge: Harvard University Press, 1985), 224.

[40]Ibid., 246.

[41]Brian M. Jenkins and Janera Johnson, *International Terrorism: A Chronology, 1968-1974* (Department of State/Defense Advanced Research Projects Agency Report, Santa Monica, CA: RAND), 34.

[42]Stefan H. Leader, "The Rise of Terrorism," *Security Management Magazine*, April 1997, 2.

[43]Phillip Wilcox, transcript of a State Department briefing to release *Patterns of Global Terrorism 1996* (Washington, DC: U.S. Department of State, 30 April 1997), 1.

[44]Patricia Chisholm, "Japan's Nightmare," *Maclean's*, 29 May 1995, 39.

[45]Phillip Wilcox, *Patterns of Global Terrorism Report* (Washington, DC: U.S. Department of State, 30 April 1997), 1.

[46]Clinton, *U.S. Policy on Counterterrorism*, 4.

[47]DoD Directive 2000.12, 6.

[48]Ibid., 8.

[49]DoD 0-2000.12-H, 4-2.

[50]CJCSH 5260, 10.

[51]DoD 0-2000.12-H, 4-4.

[52]CJCSH 5260, 10.

[53]CJCSH 5260, 16.

[54]FM 100-5, 2-5.

[55]U.S. Navy, NDP 2, *Naval Intelligence (Washington, DC: Department of the Navy, 30 September 1994)*, 24.

CHAPTER 5

CASE STUDIES

Using the previous two chapters as a backdrop, it is instructional to apply the current

doctrine to the selected case studies, the 1982 Beirut bombing and the 1996 Khobar Towers

attack. This will help resolve whether or not the doctrine could reasonably be expected to prevent

a repeat of a similar incident.

1983 Beirut International Airport Bombing

On 29 September 1982, U.S. military forces deployed to Lebanon as part of a

multinational force (USMNF) composed of French, Italian, and eventually British troops. This

force was designed to set the conditions for the withdrawal of foreign forces (mostly Israeli and

Syrian troops) and allow the Government of Lebanon to reassert control and sovereignty over

Beirut by using the Lebanese Armed Forces. The operation was intended to be a short-duration

deployment. Initially, U.S. forces received a friendly welcome as impartial guarantors of peace.

The environment was to deteriorate rapidly over the next six months. American

involvement to escalated to the point where the National Security Council directed the U.S. Navy

to provide offshore naval gunfire in an attempt to stabilize the situation. Such actions proved

counterproductive and soon the U.S. was perceived to have lost its neutrality by appearing too

pro-Israeli and too anti-Muslim. Consequently, the U.S. embassy in Beirut was destroyed by a

terrorist car bomb on April 18, 1983. By August of that year, the American positions at the

Beirut International Airport were under intermittent fire and car bombings and sniper activity was

on the rise.

On 23 October 1983, a suicide bomber driving a truck loaded with an estimated

equivalent of 12,000 pounds of TNT forced its way through the perimeter of the main U.S.

headquarters at the International Airport. The truck penetrated the building containing the

Marine's Battalion Landing Team (BLT) Headquarters and detonated. The explosion completely destroyed the building and killed 241 U.S. military members.[1]

The Secretary of Defense tasked Admiral Robert L. J. Long (retired) to establish a commission to conduct an investigation. The commission examined the mission of the U.S. Marines, the rules of engagement, the responsiveness of the chain of command, the intelligence support, the security measures enacted, and casualty handling (further discussion omitted).

Before going into the findings in detail, its important to present the chain of command at the time of the bombing because two of the commission's findings indict various aspects of the chain of command. This chain ran from the President and the Secretary of Defense (the National Command Authority or NCA) to the Commander in Chief of the United States European Command (USCINCEUR). USCINEUR assigned the mission to the Commander United States Naval Forces Europe, CINCUSNAVEUR, who in turn delegated the mission to the commander of the United States Sixth Fleet (COMSIXTHFLT), the U.S. Mediterranean naval command and designated the command as Combined Task Force 61. COMSIXTHFLT in turn designated the commander of his amphibious task force as the commander of CTF 61. Since this commander stayed aboard the USS *Austin*, it was necessary to assign an on-scene commander and CTF 62 (Commander U.S. Forces Ashore Lebanon) was designated. The chain is depicted in figure 5.

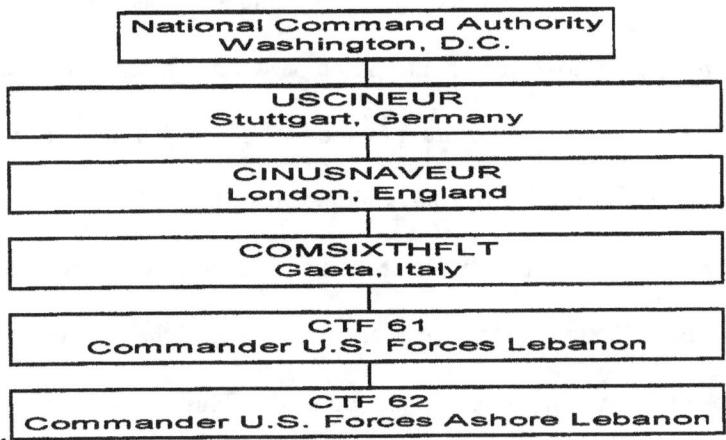

Figure 5. Beirut Chain of Command

Finding 1. Confusion about the military mission and mission creep in a changing environment. The Long Commission's first relevant conclusion was observing the considerable confusion on the part of the chain of command as to the mission of the USMNF. The apparent disconnect extended to the highest levels of the national security apparatus. After the decision was made to introduce American troops into Lebanon, the Joint Chiefs of Staff collaborated with USCINCEUR to develop a mission statement "that remained within the limits of the national political guidance."[2] This mission statement was sent to USCINCEUR in the form of a JCS Alert Order and read as follows: "To establish an environment which will permit the Lebanese Armed Forces to carry out their responsibilities in the Beirut area. When directed, USCINCEUR will introduce U.S. forces as part of a multinational force presence in the Beirut area to occupy and secure positions along a designated section of the line from south of the Beirut International Airport to a position in the vicinity of the Presidential Palace; be prepared to protect U.S. forces; and, on order, conduct retrograde operations as required."[3]

As this mission statement worked its way down the chain of command, being modified and adopted for the applicable units, the term "presence" was subject to varying interpretations. In addition, the JCS Alert Order also included guidance that the USMNF would not be engaged in combat. Peacetime rules of engagement would apply and USCINCEUR would be prepared to extract the U.S. forces in the face of hostile action. This guidance was commensurate with forces conducting peacekeeping operations; forces interposed between factions with the approval of the warring parties. As previously stated, the situation the U.S. forces found themselves in thirteen months after their introduction (the time of the bombing) was decidedly not a peacekeeping operation--it was more akin to combat. By October, the U.S. forces were the constant recipients of sniper fire, bomb attacks, and mortar and artillery fire. This led the on-scene commander to consolidate his troops in the building subsequently attacked. This structure was known to be extremely resistant to the type of artillery and sniper fire they had been receiving.

The four changes to the mission statement, mostly administrative in nature, that were promulgated from the JCS did nothing to recognize this fundamental change in the environment. The mission, still officially one of "presence" was no longer grounded in anything resembling reality. Mission creep, an insidious evolution of the role of the U.S. forces, had occurred and the chain of command did not revise the primary assumptions the mission was based on.

How does this relate to U.S. forces today? Military leaders expect this type of scenario to replay itself over and over. Often, commanders can be introduced into situations without a clear understanding of the environment and the mission. As time passes, the original conditions change substantially and the original assumptions and guidance must be reviewed and revised as necessary. Current examples include the recent experience in Somalia and the ongoing missions in Bosnia and Haiti.

Two remedies have been offered to this problem vis-à-vis the environmental and operational doctrine. As pointed out earlier, CJCSH 5260 demands the protection of U.S. soldiers in all locations and situations. Therefore, in the antiterrorism perspective it doesn't really matter what the mission was or that it suffered from mission creep. The commander has the inherent, full time responsibility for antiterrorism activities. From the outset, commanders must consider possible terrorist attacks and plan accordingly. The key is for the commander to have the correct mindset, which is established by solid environmental doctrine that demands AT activities across the spectrum. Any inconsistencies with this philosophy in the doctrine must be corrected.

The second solution is the doctrinal requirement promulgated by DOD Directive 2000.12 for the theater CINC to review security precautions at all military activities for compliance with the directive's accompanying DoD 0-2000.12-H. Such a review would have highlighted the fundamental change in mission to the higher echelons and prompted security changes had the commander already not undertaken the required action.

<u>Finding 2. The Rules of Engagement (ROE) were not properly structured</u>. The importance of a clear, easily remembered set of rules to guide the action of the private on the ground cannot be understated. The commission's findings included a statement: "The Commission concludes that a single set of ROE . . . had not been provided to, nor implemented by, CTF 62. The Commission further concludes that the mission statement, the original ROE, and the implementation in May 1983 of dual "Blue Card--White Card" ROE contributed to the mindset that detracted from the readiness of the USMNF to respond to the terrorist threat which materialized on 23 October 1983."[4]

The "Blue Card--White Card" ROE the Commission refers to is a system devised by the CTF 62 (the ground commander) to implement a dual security system. A "White Card" printed with a particular set of rules would delineate the ROE for most of the USMNF members, excluding those on a special security mission. This set of ROE was extremely restricted and geared to the original permissive peacekeeping mission with an associated minimal use of force. The commission concluded this set of ROE were "neither effective nor adequate. That event [the embassy bombing] clearly signaled a change in the environment: the employment of terrorist tactics by hostile elements."[5]

The "Blue Card" ROE was issued by USCINCEUR in the aftermath of the April embassy bombing. It was geared for those providing security for the American diplomatic community and was considered much more aggressive, especially in identifying and engaging targets perceived as showing hostile intent. The CTF 62 commander believed that these ROE could only be applied if engaged in the specific security mission. And while both sets of ROE specifically allowed for self-defense on the part of individual members of the USMNF, the "White Card" was especially restrictive in defining a hostile act.

To summarize this condition, at the time of the attack on the barracks the individual on the ground could be operating under one of two sets of rules. That individual, placed in an uncertain situation and most likely under stress, would be required to mentally sort out which rules applied and act decisively.

This finding again has relevance to the environmental and operational doctrine. Most importantly, the fact that there were two sets of ROE shows the entire chain of command did not comprehend the operating environment and did not design a single system to operate across the continuum. Fortunately, the solution to this problem has already been implemented in the form of the Joint Chiefs of Staff Standing ROE. This set of rules form the basis of any operation across the spectrum and can be made more restrictive by the chain of command. The one element that is never compromised is the inherent right of all American soldiers to protect themselves and their force from "an actual or imminent threat of attack."[6] This understanding should preclude a similar problem in the future.

This finding also has relevance at the organizational and tactical levels. With different standards promulgated by the different services, it is very likely that an Air Force sentry would react differently than a Marine sentry in the same circumstances. This condition points out the need for a DoD standard in regard to this level of doctrine. This would reinforce the "train like you will fight" mindset necessary for successful joint and multinational military operations.

Finding 3. The Responsibility of the Chain of Command. The Commission also investigated the exercise of command responsibility by the chain of command. This chain was fairly clean, as depicted before. Still, the Commission found little oversight by higher echelons to CTF 62 in regards to force protection. "In fact, the Commission's inquiry revealed a general attitude throughout the chain of command that security measures in effect ashore were essentially the sole province of the USMNF Commander and that it would somehow be improper to tell him how best to protect his force."[7]

While it is important to preserve the commanders' prerogative to exercise judgement, it is equally important for the superiors in the chain of command to provide guidance and assistance.

Military operations today are complex and demand considerable attention to detail. To prevent the on-scene commander from inadvertently overlooking vulnerabilities, today's doctrine contains a system of checks and balances. For example, the most important role in preventing terrorist attacks in this environment, other than that of the field commander, belongs to the theater CINC. CINCs under joint doctrine are tasked to assess the command relationships for each subordinate command to ensure adequate protection from terrorist attack. Today, it is clear that AT responsibilities exist all along the chain of command. This is not to impede the on-scene commanders or usurp their authority, but to provide additional resources and expertise to assist those commanders. A final note, the command relationship assessment is done on a periodic basis for joint task forces. This is a wise policy in that the personnel turnover rate in joint task forces is notoriously high and periodic updates will counter the loss in expertise caused by personnel rotation. This attention by the chain of command should preclude recurrence.

Finding 4. Intelligence Shortfalls. Intelligence support to the commander was found lacking. Although the Commission found documented evidence of the receipt of a large number of intelligence warnings regarding terrorist threats, the commander "was not provided with timely intelligence, tailored to his specific operational needs."[8] Recognizing the limited human intelligence capability inherent in the military, the report calls for increased interagency cooperation, specifically between the DoD and the Central Intelligence Agency.

This finding has implications across the entire doctrinal spectrum. It seems to be a maxim of military operations that intelligence on the enemy's capabilities and intentions will always be incomplete. Even if that is true, American forces must strive for the best possible intelligence at all times; one crucial piece of timely information could prevent disasters of this type.

Finding 5. The Security Measures Enacted. This section outlines in detail the activities of the Marines leading up to the catastrophe. It chronicles the tactical operations that went into the force protection effort. While these are not subject to analysis in this study, it is important to note that only in the aftermath of the next case study (the Khobar Towers incident) did the DoD adopt standard physical security measures. It remains to be seen if those measures will be adequately applied and successful in preventing further tragedies.

Other fundamental and strategic implications. This attack was an impetus for commissioning the vice president to issue the report that is still referred to in a majority of the literature. From a fundamental standpoint, the doctrine today can adequately address this scenario. Set in the history of the Middle East, it is obvious (and not just in hindsight) that the presence of the Marines in Beirut was a quintessential target in the underlying nature of warfare by terrorism. This fact has not changed, nor will it change in the foreseeable future.

Other environmental and operational considerations. Applying today's doctrine to this attack shows significant shortfalls still exist at this level. Most significant is the lack of consistency in describing the requirement for AT activities at every turn. Standing rules of engagement and improvements in intelligence capabilities are positive outcomes of this tragedy, but the intelligence issue will be revisited in the next case study.

Finally with regard to the restraints discussed in the previous chapter, U.S. forces are normally deployed with an understanding of the host nation responsibilities for security. The Long Commission stated their belief that the security of the USMNF was conditional and that "the Lebanese Armed Forces would provide for the security of the areas in which the force was to operate."[9] Unfortunately, American forces were placed in a situation where the host country could do little to assist in their security. The only way to resolve this dilemma in the future is to either evacuate the force if the host nation is incapable of meeting their obligations or provide sufficient force structure as to obviate the need for host nation support. The introduction of a heavy U.S. armor force into Bosnia is an excellent example of self-reliance in the absence of host nation support.

1996 Khobar Towers Bombing

On 25 June, 1996, shortly before 10:00 p.m. local time. a fuel truck loaded with the equivalent of 3,000- to 8,000 pounds of TNT pulled up next to the northern perimeter fence of the Khobar Towers complex in Dhahran, Saudi Arabia. The government of Saudi Arabia provided the Towers to house U.S. and coalition forces enforcing the no-fly ban over southern Iraq dubbed Operation SOUTHERN WATCH. Over 3,000 Americans, mostly Air Force members temporarily assigned to the 4404th Wing (Provisional), were billeted there. The drivers of the truck fled immediately in a getaway car. An alert sentry noticed the activity and immediately began to evacuate Building 131, the one closest to the truck. Unfortunately, the evacuation was still in progress minutes later when the truck exploded. The blast sheared off the north face of the building and caused hundreds of windows to shatter, turning the shards of flying glass into deadly airborne projectiles.

In the end, the human cost was 19 dead and almost 500 wounded. The command would require almost three days to reconstitute its forces to accomplish the assigned mission. There was one other casualty that would take until July of 1997 to manifest. On 31 July, almost 13 months after the attack, Secretary of Defense William Cohen, with the concurrence of President Clinton and General John Shalikashvili, the CJCS, announced he had blocked the promotion of the Air Force commander at the time of the bombing, Brigadier General Terryl Schwalier, to the rank of Major General.

In the aftermath of the bombing, then-Secretary of Defense William Perry commissioned retired General Wayne Downing to issue a report on the incident. General Downing outlines eight major findings with respect to antiterrorism; it is incumbent to note the lack of clear, comprehensive doctrine is prominent in seven of the eight findings.

Finding 1. A Comprehensive Approach to Force Protection is Required. In a very

significant portion of the report, General Downing calls for an integrated approach to

antiterrorism:

> The Assessment Task Force recommended that the Department of Defense take a range
> of actions to deter, prevent, or mitigate the effects of future terrorist attacks on
> servicemen and women overseas. None will--in and of themselves--provide an
> environment secure from all potential threats. However, the Task Force strongly believes
> that to assure an acceptable level of security for U.S. forces worldwide, commanders
> must aggressively pursue an integrated systems approach to force protection that combine
> awareness and training, physical security measures, advanced technology systems, and
> specific protection measure tailored to each location.[10]

Only adequate doctrine can make this possible.

Finding 2. DoD Must Establish Force Protection Standards. Recognizing the need for

guidance and standardization across the DoD spectrum, the Task Force called on the DoD to

provide sufficient information to the local commander: "While all U.S. commanders in the Gulf

thought they had sufficient resources for force protection, they were not knowledgeable of

technologies to enhance protection or how to develop an integrated systems approach to security.

Consequently, they underestimated true requirements."[11]

In other words, commanders do not know what they do not know. In response to this

finding, a search of the doctrine reveals only the Air Force's organizational doctrine discusses

this systems approach to solving the problem.

Only a two-pronged, "push-pull" approach will work to resolve this issue. DoD must

"push" relevant information to commanders using a variety of techniques and technologies, and

commanders must develop a critical thinking methodology in order to "pull" required information

from their staffs and support agencies.

A positive outcome of this finding was to set the AT standards in the DoD 0-2000.12-H

as the norm for all services and CINCs. While subordinate commanders could make the requirements more restrictive, deviations from the standards could only occur with appropriate approval.

Finding 3. U.S. Central Command Requires an Empowered Chain of Command in the Region. General Downing uses this finding to point out a fundamental flaw in command relationship structures common in contingency operations. In the SOUTHERN WATCH situation, as well as many other joint task force (JTF) organizations, the JTF had tactical control and oversight of the forces, but the CONUS-based service component headquarters retained operational control. The point was brought up in the report, "The DoD must clarify command relationships in U.S. Central Command to ensure that all commanders have the requisite authority to accomplish their assigned responsibilities."[12] It is also important to note the report calls for commanders to review their organization and structure of all temporary activities (like a JTF) frequently to allow change when needed. This is particularly crucial as the initial forces that established the original procedures and relationships rotate out of theater, taking the corporate knowledge (and a multitude of verbal agreements) with them.

Finding 4. Command Emphasis on and Involvement in Force Protection are Crucial. In perhaps the most telling finding of the report, General Downing was adamant about the personal attention given by commanders to the antiterrorist equation. Noting that at the time of the bombing various committees and panels were actively reviewing force protection policies and practices, those dialogues did not help the commanders with their security dilemma.

The report stated, "Committees are not effective without the emphasis and personal attention of commanders. In part, the inconsistent, and sometimes inadequate, force protection practices among service forces, joint headquarters, and different countries resulted from insufficient command involvement."[13]

With the doctrinal changes taken in the wake of this report, the U.S. military has crafted a built-in safety system in which service activities are evaluated by joint agencies under the auspices of the various CINCs.

Finding 5. The Intelligence Community Provided Warning of the Potential for a Terrorist Attack. Although the fundamental thrust of this finding was a call for more intelligence funding and resources (reminiscent of the language in the Long Commission Report) the report vindicates the intelligence community for warning commanders that the threat was increasing (although not specifically against Khobar Towers). The report does indict the intelligence community for not exploiting all the potential sources of information available to them. In relation to the commanders' role, a commander is best served by remembering the U.S. Army doctrine that commanders drive the intelligence apparatus to suit their needs. As amplified in Army FM 101-5, "The commander alone decides what information is critical, based upon his experience, the mission, the higher commander's intent, and input from the staff."[14] The commander uses the Commander's Critical Information Requirements (CCIR) method to identify those things in relation to the enemy (priority intelligence requirements or PIR), in relation to protect friendly troops (essential elements of friendly information or EEFI) and information about organic or adjacent capabilities (friendly forces information requirements (FFIR). By adapting the CCIR into the context of antiterrorism, commanders have a ready-made methodology for the efficient use of their intelligence apparatus in an antiterrorism role.

Finding 6. The Chain of Command Was Responsible for Protecting the Forces at Khobar Towers. In this portion of the report, General Downing was very critical of the command structure in general and the Air Force commander's actions in particular. There are three particular comments that bear closer scrutiny.

First, the command relationships established in the region did not support unity of effort in force protection. Second, there were no force protection or training standards provided by U.S.

Central command to forces assigned or deployed to the theater. Third, the rotation and manning policies established by the U.S. Air Force did not support complete, cohesive units (especially Security Police) who were capable of coping with a viable terrorist threat.[15]

The first point has been discussed previously. In current terms, this statement by General Downing reinforces the importance of an involved chain of command.

The second point led to the designation of the DoD 0-2000.12-H as the force protection standard. Setting worldwide standards that can be augmented to meet local conditions should mitigate the problem.

As a partial response to the final comment, the Air Force has developed an organizational structure known as the air expeditionary force capable of deploying a mission-tailored force package, complete with an integral force protection group, to hotspots around the world. This package would institutionalize AT doctrine and would create significantly enhanced continuity as forces are rotated through the contingency.

Finding 7. Host Nations Share in the Responsibility for Force Protection. Agreements to station American forces on another sovereign's territory are usually worked at the highest diplomatic levels. Sensitivity on the part of both the host nation's populous to having "foreign" soldiers on their soil and the American public's aversion to foreign entanglements often require compromise and conciliation on everyone's part. Commanders' concerns over force protection issues may directly clash with diplomatic or political concerns. The Downing Report indicates the best ways to avoid these conflicts are for the commander to set the tone in U.S. and host nation relations: "Host nations have responsibility for the security of U.S. service members and installations in their country. The option of locating forces in isolated areas may not always exist. U.S. commanders and staffs must appreciate the importance of positive, working relationships with their host nation counterparts for force protection. Through these relationships, they can influence selection of locations of installations, allocation of host-nation guard forces and priorities, and enhancement of host nation security as the threat conditions escalate."[16]

A seemingly significant problem with this approach is the lack of authority and the reliance on a commander's "influence" to accomplish appropriate force protection measures. In a situation where a commander is actively blocked by the host-nation counterpart in implementing needed procedures or measures, the commander walks a fine line in maintaining relations while elevating the issue for diplomatic resolution at higher levels. There can be a natural reluctance on the part of a commander to elevate issues that may prove to be a diplomatic bombshell. That said, the bottom line is that commanders never abrogate their responsibilities while on foreign soil.

Finding 8. Department of State/Department of Defense Division of Responsibility Does Not Provide U.S. Forces Adequate Force Protection. This finding was prompted by the apparent disconnect in responsibilities assigned to the two Departments. A memorandum of understanding between the two assigned the force protection requirements to the senior State Department representative in country. With such a large deployment of American forces to Saudi Arabia, it was not realistic to expect the State Department's Chief of Mission to possess the resources necessary to protect such a large force. Furthermore, some deployed forces were not assigned to either the combatant commander or the Chief of Mission. While the latter oversight did not contribute to the Khobar Towers tragedy, the oversight did present a vulnerable seam in the force protection umbrella.

Summary of Case Studies

When compared side by side, the two case studies share three similarities. First, the chain of command was indicted in both cases. The fault was in the lack of proactive support, responsiveness, emphasis on force protection, and a comprehension that AT responsibilities exist at every echelon of command. While command responsibilities are generally well delineated in the doctrine today, military members must forever be on the guard against units or individuals that have the potential to miss being shaded by the doctrinal tree.

Second, intelligence support was cited in both cases as contributing to the events. Successful AT efforts must be anchored in intelligence from all levels and all sources that meet the needs of the commander. Lieutenant Colonel Pangman expressed it well, "The Long Commission which investigated the 1983 Beirut bombing found that U.S. human intelligence and counterintelligence capabilities had eroded. The commission recommended that immediate actions to address this significant shortfall be taken. Yet, 13 years later, the Downing investigation of the Khobar Towers bombing identified the same shortcomings and recommended essentially the same fix."[17]

The final commonality was a call for standardized, DoD-wide force protection measures. To reiterate, the response by the Secretary of Defense was to designate the measures in the DoD 0-2000.12-H as the worldwide standard. This is probably the most beneficial outcome of the incidents. Having a common framework will allow all the forces operating in the same environment to gain unity of effort and synergism in defeating terrorism.

---

[1]Long, 3.

[2]Ibid., 35.

[3]Ibid., 40.

[4]Ibid., 51.

[5]Ibid., 47.

[6]Joint Staff, *Joint Task Force Commander's Handbook for Peace Operations* (Washington, DC: DoD, 29 April 1994), 75.

[7]Long, 54.

[8]Ibid., 9.

[9]Ibid., 43.

[10]Downing, 4.

[11]Ibid., 4.

[12]Ibid., 5.

[13]Ibid., 6.

[14]U.S. Army, Field Manual 101-5, *Staff Organization and Operations* (Washington, DC: Department of the Army, 31 May 1997), 5-8.

[15]Downing, 6.

[16]Ibid.

[17]Dale Pangman, "Can the U.S. Adequately Protect its Forces?" (Newport, RI: Naval War College, 13 June 1997), 3.

CHAPTER 6

CONCLUSIONS AND RECOMMENDATIONS

At the beginning this thesis set about to answer a series of questions, the answers to which would combine to reveal the shortfalls and recommended reforms for the current antiterrorism doctrine.

First to be discovered was how doctrine was defined and amplification of its prominent characteristics. In the most significant result of this segment of the analysis, the evidence showed the four different military services have varying definitions of the term. The controversy is a visible divergence regarding the authoritative or directive nature of doctrine. In the complex joint and multinational environment American forces will most likely operate in, how can there be such a diversity of views on the fundamental basis for all military actions? Therefore, the first recommendation from this study is that consensus must be reached on the very definition of doctrine. The author recommends this as an appropriate avenue of future research.

The next question asked was if the current doctrine could be described in the context of a fundamental, environmental, and organizational framework. This would give structure to the study as well as set the conditions for observing deficiencies. The analysis was successful in identifying applicable doctrine at all three levels. For the most part, the fundamental doctrine was shown to contain basic beliefs about terrorism and antiterrorism (AT), had a timeless quality, and was not invalidated by changing political winds or obsolescence caused by rapid changes in technology.

At the environment level, some discrepancies came to light. It was quite clear that the fundamental doctrine reinforces the environmental requirement that AT efforts be an integral part of everything the military does. Unfortunately, there did not emerge a clear picture of a consistent environmental basis that described AT as necessary under all conditions and at all times. Usually, antiterrorism was described as a separate, discrete operation under the auspices of

86

military operations other than war. Also contributing to that perception is the assignment of AT

policymaking to the primary purview of the Assistant Secretary of Defense, Special

Operations/Low Intensity Conflict (ASD/SOLIC), presumably relegating AT to something other

than conventional military activities. That is not to say that proponency for AT should not reside

with ASD/SOLIC; it is a logical meld with the office's other combatting terrorism

responsibilities. It merely indicates that when the two factors are combined, the perception

encourages the wrong mindset and increases the resistance to accepting AT in the mainstream

where it belongs. Figure 6 represents a recommended revision to the extract from JP 3-0 that was

previously discussed. In order to set the correct conditions for recognizing the unfailing AT

requirement, explicit articulation of the encompassing role of AT should accompany the revised

graphic in a change to that publication.

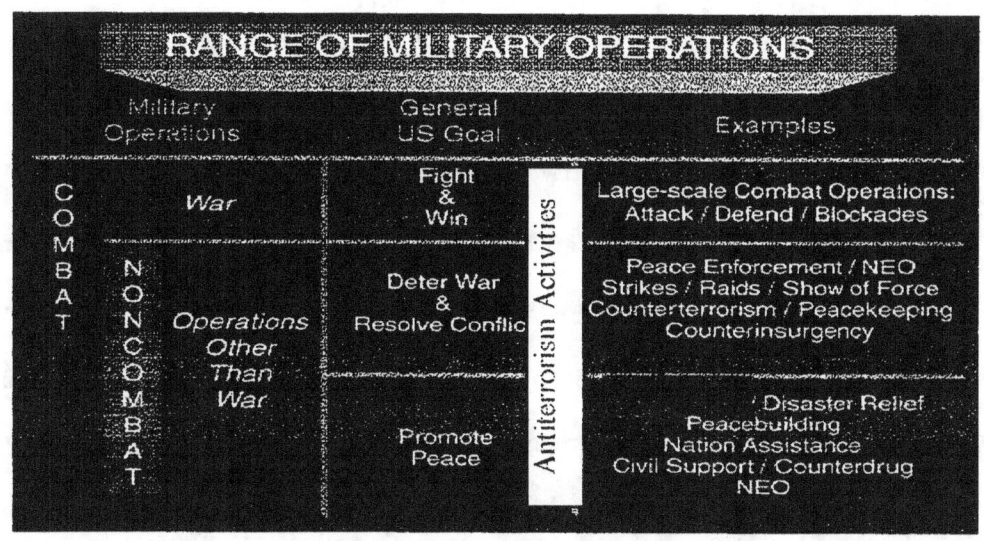

Figure I-1. Range of Military Operations

I-2   Joint Pub 3-0

Figure 6 Revised Range of Military Operations

There is a wide spectrum of AT doctrine at the organizational level, ranging from the

comprehensive to the nonexistent. As a minimum, each service must promulgate guidance at this level, even if it is to refer the commander to the relevant joint documents. Additionally, the tendency to place AT in a distinct category is prevalent here too. Again, the recommendation would be to make AT an explicit part of all operations in this category of doctrine.

Following that same hierarchical structure, the doctrine was simultaneously evaluated to determine if the content met strategic, operational, and tactical requirements. The study successfully demonstrated that the strategic doctrine adequately described an appropriate end-state. The President of the United States places considerable emphasis on providing AT protection to American military forces, an issue worthy of prominent inclusion in the presidential *Policy on Countering Terrorism* and *A National Security Strategy for a New Century*. Further, the conclusion can be reached that the Department of Defense (DoD) has issued appropriate AT objectives in the form of *The National Military Strategy*. However, when attempting to match ways and means to those objectives, there was little discernable direction to guide the prioritization of competing requirements and the programming of scarce resources. Only sound military advocacy from the Joint Chiefs of Staff coupled with strong leadership from the White House and a cooperative Congress can rectify these shortfalls.

One of the most significant observations at the operational level is the identification of a two-track military system. Seemingly, the service responsibilities to organize, train, and equip forces (under service doctrine) for employment by theater commanders-in-chief (CINCs) (under joint doctrine) can cause an invitation to struggle. Two examples are indicative. First, a CINC may recognize an AT deficiency but must rely on the appropriate service to budget sufficient funds to fix the problem. Solutions to this type of problem can only be implemented if all the concerned parties recognize and agree to the pressing need. Second, the simultaneous existence of joint and service doctrine can sow confusion. This problem will be mitigated if there is a concerted effort to write comprehensive joint doctrine that obviates the need for separate and distinct service doctrine. But in a larger sense, this duality inherently builds in a series of checks and balances between the services and the CINCs that can prove beneficial.

An equally obvious need for doctrinal reform at the operational level is the requirement for interagency and multinational AT doctrine. It is not sufficient to mandate existing doctrine as being applicable for use in such circumstances. As demonstrated repeatedly, American military forces will be expected to operate in environments with other governmental, nongovernmental, and military forces of other nations. Further development of this line of questioning is certainly warranted and should be undertaken immediately.

The excursion into the tactical realm was brief but nonetheless fruitful. In almost every case, the services did not specifically accede to the mandated DoD standard. Rapid compliance is essential in order to have standard protections.

The AT doctrinal tree is rooted in the need to understand the threat. This threat is undergoing a metamorphosis into a more violent, dangerous and indiscriminant danger to American forces. Commanders must align all their intelligence functions to assess that threat so that proper measures can be implemented. The doctrine contains a model suitable for such a task, but training and education would be required to realize its capabilities.

To fully appreciate the problem faced by commanders in their daily activities, an overview of the doctrinal restrictions, constraints, and limits placed on their authority to combat terrorism was presented. Commanders have sufficient authority within the confines of their respective installations. However, under the present system commanders must work with civilian authorities and host nation officials to counter threats outside the installation. Without the requisite authority, commanders must rely on their ability to influence the appropriate authorities so as to accomplishing the required AT efforts.

Commanders must also make conscious, informed decisions to balance accomplishing the assigned mission with effective antiterrorism measures. Additionally, commanders can find the materiel and personnel requirements needed for effective AT programs are competing with other issues that demand similar attention. These problems defy easy answers, but one thing is clear; commander must use the chain of command to voice their concerns and request guidance as needed. Asking for assistance from higher echelons does not diminish the confidence held by the superiors and it does not abrogate the commanders' authority, it is a responsible approach to solving the problem.

Probably the single most important change the military can make to the doctrine is to instill a necessity to incorporate the concept of force protection under the principle of security in every circumstance. The Air Force says it best, "Although joint doctrine places combatting terrorism under MOOTW, Air Force personnel need to understand that combatting terrorism is not limited to nonwar operations. It is clearly force protection and applies across the range of military operations. All Air Force personnel need to actively protect themselves and their units from terrorism. This is particularly true for personnel in high-risk areas but should never be taken lightly anywhere."[1]

The similarities of the case studies could lead us to a dangerous presumption. It is the presumption that the military is destined to repeat the failures of the past. After the Beirut attack the Long Commission concluded, "that much needs to be done to prepare U.S. military forces to defend against and counter terrorism."[2] Compared with a conclusion of the Downing report thirteen years later, "The Department of Defense can more effectively protect our men and women around the world. I am concerned that insufficient attention is being given to antiterrorism and force protection."[3] The similarities are disturbing, for one could discern a chronic form of institutional amnesia. Fortunately, the cure for this collective amnesia is found in robust doctrine that is in a constant state of evolution: "It must be emphasized that doctrine development is never complete. Innovation has always been a key part of sound doctrinal development and must continue to play a central role. Doctrine is constantly changing as new experiences and advances in technology point the way to the force of the future."[4]

---

[1]U.S. Air Force, AFDD 2-3, *Military Operations Other Than War* (Washington, DC: Department of the Air Force, 5 October 1996), 25.

[2]Long, 141.

[3]Downing, x.

[4]AFDD 1, 2.

BIBLIOGRAPHY

Books

Ford, Franklin L. *Political Murder: From Tyrannicide to Terrorism.* Cambridge: Harvard University Press, 1985.

Alexander, Yonah, and Walter Laqueur, ed. *The Terrorism Reader: The Essential Source Book on Political Violence Both Past and Present.* New York: Penguin, 1987.

Laqueur, Walter. *Terrorism: A Study of National and International Violence.* Boston: Little, Brown and Company, 1977.

Merari, Ariel, ed. *On Terrorism and Combating Terrorism.* Frederick: University Publications of America, 1985.

Mickolus, Edward F., Jean M. Murdock, and Todd Sandler. *International Terrorism in the 1980s: A Chronology of Events Volume II.* Ames: Iowa State University Press, 1989.

Seger, Karl A. *The Antiterrorism Handbook.* Novato: Presidio Press, 1990.

Sloan, Stephen. *Beating International Terrorism: An Action Strategy for Preemption and Punishment.* Maxwell Air Force Base: Air University Press, 1986.

Government Documents

Assistant Secretary of Defense (Special Operations/Low Intensity Conflict). DoD 0-2000-12-H, *Protection of DoD Personnel and Activities Against Acts of Terrorism and Political Turbulence.* Washington, DC: Department of Defense, February 1993.

Bush, George, Vice President. *Public Report of the Vice President's Task Force of Combatting Terrorism.* Washington, DC: The White House, February 1986.

Chairman of the Joint Chiefs of Staff. CJCS Handbook 5260, *Commander's Handbook for Antiterrorism Readiness.* Washington, DC: Department of Defense, 1 January 1997.

_____. *Joint Vision 2010.* Washington, DC: Department of Defense, undated.

_____. *National Military Strategy of the Unites States of America.* Washington, DC: Department of Defense, 1997.

Clinton, William J., President. *A National Security Strategy for a New Century.* Washington, DC: The White House, May 1997.

_____. Presidential Decision Directive 39, *U.S. Policy of Counterterrorism.* Washington, DC: The White House, 21 June 1995.

Commandant of the Marine Corps. *General Orders for Sentries.* Washington, DC: United States Marine Corps, undated.

_____. Fleet Marine Force Reference Publication 7-14A, *The Individual's Guide for Understanding and Surviving Terrorism.* Washington, DC: United States Marine Corps, 31 October 1987.

_____. Marine Corps Order 3301.1, *Combatting Terrorism/Internal Security Plan for Headquarters Marine Corp.* Washington, DC: United States Marine Corps, 15 January 1992.

Downing, Wayne A. *Report of the Assessment of the Khobar Towers Bombing.* Washington, DC: Department of Defense, 30 August 1996.

Jenkins, Brian M. and Janera Johnson. *International Terrorism: A Chronology, 1968-1974.* Santa Monica, RAND Corporation, 1975.

Joint Staff. *The Joint Doctrine Story.* Washington, DC: Joint Staff J-7 Directorate, undated.

_____. JP 3-0, *Doctrine for Joint Operations.* Washington, DC: Department of Defense, 1 February 1995.

_____. JP 3-07, *Joint Doctrine for Military Operations Other Than War.* Washington, DC: Department of Defense, 16 June 1995.

_____. JP 3-07.2, *Joint Tactics, Techniques and Procedures for Antiterrorism.* Washington, DC: Department of Defense, 25 June 1993.

_____. Joint Staff Pamphlet 5260, *Coping with Violence: Personal Protection Pamphlet.* Washington, DC: Department of Defense, July 1996.

Long, Robert L. J. *Report of the DoD Commission on Beirut International Airport Terrorist Act, October 23, 1983.* Washington, DC: Department of Defense, 20 December 1983.

Perry, William J. *Report to the President and Congress on the Protection of U.S. Forces Deployed Abroad.* Washington, DC: Office of the Secretary of Defense, 15 September, 1996.

Secretary of Defense. DoD Directive 2000.12, *DoD Combating Terrorism Program.* Washington, DC: Department of Defense, September 1996.

U.S. Air Force, Air Force Doctrine Document 1, *Basic Doctrine.* Washington, DC: Department of the Air Force, September 1997.

_____. Air Force Doctrine Document 2-3, *Military Operations Other than War.* Washington, DC: Department of the Air Force, 5 October 1996.

_____. Air Force Instruction 31-210, *The Air Force Antiterrorism (AT) Program.* Washington, DC: Department of the Air Force, July 1997.

U.S. Army. Field Manual 100-5, *Operations.* Washington, DC: Department of the Army, June 1993.

_____. Field Manual 101-5, *Staff Organization and Operations.* Washington, DC: Department of the Army, 31 May 1997.

_____. Field Manual 101-5-1, *Operational Terms and Graphics.* Washington, DC: Department of the Army, 30 September 1997.

_____. Army Regulation 525-13, *The Army Combatting Terrorism Program.* Washington, DC: Department of the Army, July 1992.

U.S. Department of State, *Patterns of Global Terrorism 1996.* Washington, DC: Department of State, 1996.

U.S. General Accounting Office, *Combating Terrorism: Status of DoD Efforts to Protect Its Forces Overseas.* Washington, DC: GAO, 1997

U.S. Navy. Naval Doctrinal Publication 1, *Naval Warfare.* Washington, DC: Department of the Navy, 18 March 1994.

_____. Naval Doctrinal Publication 2, *Naval Intelligence.* Washington, DC: Department of the Navy, 30 September 1994.

_____. U.S. Navy OPNAVINST 5530.15A, *Physical Security.* Washington, DC: Department of the Navy, June 1991.

Periodicals and Articles

Clinton, William. "Remarks and Statement by the President at Signing of Antiterrorism Bill." Washington, DC: The White House, 24 April 1996, 1-3.

Deutch, John. "Terrorism." *Foreign Policy*, September/October 1997, 10-22.

Drew, Dennis. "Of Trees and Leaves: A New View of Doctrine." *Air University Review*, January-February 1982, 40-48.

Goodman, Glenn W., Jr. "Countering Terrorism: An Interview with the Honorable H. Allen Holmes." *Armed Forces Journal International*, February 1998, 36-37.

Laqueur, Walter. "Postmodern Terrorism." *Foreign Affairs*, September/October 1996, 24-33.

_____. "Terrorism, Looking to the Future." *Washington*, October 1996, 9-14.

Phillips, James. "The Changing Face of Middle East Terrorism." *Heritage Foundation Backgrounder*, 6 October 1994, 1-12.

Wilkinson, Paul. "Terrorism: Motivations and Causes." *Canadian Security Intelligence Service Commentary No. 53*, January, 1995, 1-5.

Unpublished Materials and Other Sources

Bodrero, D. Douglas. "Changing the Mindset on AT--Police Perspective." Washington, DC: Department of Defense Antiterrorism Conference, September 1996. Photocopied.

Cottrell, Scott C., Major, U.S.A. "Identifying the Roles of the Separate Governmental Agencies in Countering the Proliferation of Weapons of Mass Destruction Among Nonstate Actors Throughout the Counterproliferation Continuum." Masters thesis, U.S. Army Command and General Staff College, 1997.

Haskins, Casey P., Major, U.S.A. "Turning the Tables: U.S. Strategy to Cope with Enemies Who Are Not Governments." Masters thesis, U.S. Army Command and General Staff College, 1996.

Pangman, Dale, Lieutenant Colonel, U.S.A.F., "Can the U.S. Adequately Protect Its Forces?" Monograph, U.S. Naval War College, 1977.

www.ingramcontent.com/pod-product-compliance
Lightning Source LLC
Chambersburg PA
CBHW081227280526
45787CB00006B/2559